A Good Life

A Good Life

ROBIN VOELCKER

StoryTerrace

CONTENTS

PREFACE

The main purpose of this book is to demonstrate that science, and chemistry in particular, need not be dull or boring. At the present time, chemistry is not cool. Some universities have closed their chemistry departments due to lack of demand from would-be students.

This comes at a time when we live in an increasingly scientific and technological age, so why the lack of interest? There are a number of reasons. As a profession outside academia, it is badly paid compared to other professions, has little status in the eyes of the community and is not well supported by its professional body.

There is now a growing interest from the young to save the environment, which may help people to become more interested in the sciences in the future. Currently, however, they are perceived by the young to be difficult subjects and there are certainly easier ways of obtaining a degree.

In the USA, Germany and other enlightened countries, scientists are well regarded and paid accordingly. Hence it is difficult to retain good chemistry graduates within the profession in the UK, due to low pay and poor status. I know of some who have retrained as accountants or have entered the City, where they are valued for their analytical approach and are paid accordingly. I have been asked at times, when I say I am a chemist, "What branch of Boots do you work in?" The Royal Society of Chemistry (RSC) does little to promote and explain the role of chemists, particularly to stop the confusion over chemistry and pharmacy.

Lastly, the RSC, the professional body in the UK, is run principally by academics. When I enquired why they did not support their members over pay, as the Law Society and other professional bodies do, I was told that the RSC was not a trade union and had no intention of becoming one.

My approach to writing this book is to demonstrate that the work of chemists rarely involves pure chemistry, unless you are a teacher or university lecturer. Once in a job, your expertise is applied to the chemical needs of your firm or industry. This may be far removed from what you learned at school or university.

Like graduates who left chemistry for other work, I gave up laboratory work at the age of 24 in the UK, emigrated to Southern Rhodesia and joined a multi-national conglomerate in the packaging industry as a management trainee. On many occasions I was asked to assist in problems that had occurred in one of the group's factories where an analytical approach was required.

The six years I spent in Africa gave me management experience at a younger age than would have been possible in the UK. This experience resulted in me being offered jobs by two of the big four management consulting firms when

I returned to the UK. After four years as a management consultant, I decided with a friend to branch out on our own. My father had a small consultancy that was almost bankrupt, so I used it as the vehicle for our venture.

We took our new business into the fields of the environment and food safety. We were assisted in this by the Control of Pollution Act, which came into force in 1974. We knew we were on the right track, and at the same time it was gratifying to be returning to our roots. We built up the practice and sold it in 1998 to one of the privatised water companies.

In the book, each chapter is complete in itself and mainly describes projects carried out for clients. Some chapters explain the chemistry involved. The projects were undertaken mainly from 1962 to 1982, apart from the chapter on tobacco and one on the effects of the Kobe earthquake in Japan in 1996. In some cases client names have been omitted or changed.

1

A BLITZ BOYHOOD

My parents may never have married if my maternal grandparents had been able to choose a husband for my mother. They weren't keen on their daughter Carmen becoming the wife of a half German. Although my father, Eric, was born in London, his father was German born, while his mother was a lowland Scot. So I am one quarter German.

My mother's parents were also a mixture. My maternal grandfather was a medical doctor from Liverpool and my grandmother was a Highland Scot, distantly related to the Bowes-Lyon family, her maiden name being Lyon.

Although Scottish, my mother's family grew up in Valparaiso, Chile. Her great-grandfather was an engineer who had gone out there to help build the railways. Despite my mother's first language being Spanish and my father having a good command of German, neither parent taught myself or my two brothers either language, which I always regretted.

After the end of World War One, my mother's family left Chile and came to live in London. My mother was in her early 20s when she met my father, somewhere in Kensington, possibly in the Royal Palace Hotel where young people would gather to socialise and dance to the live band. My father was a very good dancer. Shrewsbury educated, he was also tall, good looking and had impeccable manners, so he was very popular with the ladies. But he wasn't so popular with my mother's parents who hoped to nip the relationship in the bud by sending Carmen to Ceylon. Her two brothers were out there planting tea and, with eligible women in short supply, the hope was that she would meet someone more suitable and forget about Eric Voelcker. But it didn't work and she sailed back to England. When the ship arrived at Tilbury Docks, my father was waiting for her and they were engaged the next day.

They married in 1930 and lived in Surrey before moving to Kensington in 1938. I was born on 1 September 1935, the second of their three sons. I was aged four when war broke out on 3 September 1939. I vaguely remember that day. I was in Kensington Gardens with my elder brother David and our nanny. A man rushed up to us and said, "Have you heard? War has been declared!" A little while later, an air-raid siren went off, but no one knew what to do. Fortunately it was a false alarm.

At the outbreak of war, myself and my two brothers, together with a nanny, were sent to stay in a magnificent house 10 miles south of Carlisle. It was owned by my mother's schoolfriend and her husband, who was in the Scots Guards. The house had a full staff and I thought that this was just how I would live when I had grown up.

This was the time of the phoney war when virtually nothing happened in the way of fighting, except at sea. So in the spring of 1940 we returned to London, just in time for the Germans to overrun nearly all of western Europe.

I remember being taken to Kensington Old Town Hall to be fitted with a gas mask. My younger brother John had one with a Mickey Mouse face on it. I screamed because I wanted a similar one but, being over the age of four, wasn't allowed. So I had to make do with a small adult's size.

In late 1940 our top-floor flat in Iverna Gardens, Kensington was hit by an incendiary bomb. This type of bomb uses the thermite process ($2Al + Fe_2O^3 = 2Fe + Al_2O_3$) in which powdered aluminium is mixed with iron oxide and ignited with a magnesium wire to generate intense heat and produce molten iron. It does not explode, but bursts into flames on impact. The incendiary bomb landed in John's cot, setting fire to the flat. Fortunately he was not in it, as we were all in the basement shelter at the time, but it caused significant damage, destroying John's bedroom and part of the roof.

London was very empty at the time, many people having moved to the country and many children billeted with families outside London. It did not take long for my parents to find alternative accommodation in Campden Hill Court, also in Kensington. This time they sensibly decided to go for a ground-floor flat.

During an air raid, many tenants from upper floors congregated in our flat. The young porter, Donald, had been called up to join the army and his place had been taken by Alderson, a retired butler. He was great and always dressed like a butler, which I assumed he had done all his life. One night, at the end of a really bad raid, one of the tenants from an upper floor remembered that she had a bottle of port. Thinking that everyone would probably welcome a drink, she went upstairs to get it. My mother, meanwhile, went to the kitchen to fetch some glasses. Alderson took one look at them and said, "Madam, those are sherry glasses." A good butler would never let anything interfere with his impeccable standards, not even a war.

Britain continued to be bombed, but thanks to the young pilots of the RAF, the Battle of Britain had conquered the threat of war on our soil. Trafalgar Square was bombed, destroying Hamptons furniture store. The western extension to the National Gallery now stands on that site.

I remember being taken in 1942 to Trafalgar Square to listen to the bells of Saint Martin-in-the-Fields church being rung for the first time in two years. At the start of the war, Churchill had ordered that church bells should not be rung as normal. They would be reserved to signal that the Germans were invading the country. Now that the invasion threat had gone away, it was safe to ring the bells again.

In 1943, at the age of seven, I went to Colet Court, the day junior school for St Paul's. The original Colet Court building in West Kensington had been taken over as the war headquarters of General Montgomery, a former St Paul's pupil.

So when I first went there it was operating from a house in Brook Green, west London. I found the whole idea to be frightening and I remember with a shudder my form teacher Mr Lee. He would enter the room swishing a cane. After placing the cane carefully on two brass uprights fixed to the top of his high desk, he would look around at us and say, "I will not hesitate to use it if anyone misbehaves." He had the reputation of doing just that. It was some time later that I realised the man was a complete sadist.

The school then transferred to Colet House in the Talgarth Road, later demolished to make way for the Cromwell Road Extension. There was a totally different atmosphere here and the great news for all of us was that Mr Lee was no longer a teacher there. I hoped he had been sacked. The teaching standards in the new building were excellent and I really took to learning maths, French and Latin.

My mother had told me to return home from school by the number 9 bus. If, however, a raid started, I should come back by underground. On one occasion I was walking along Talgarth Road heading for the underground station. Barons

Court station at that time was closed, so I had to walk to West
Kensington station. Many of the houses en route had been
burnt out. The air raid sirens went before I had reached the
underground station and I did not know what do.

Luckily for me, there were four soldiers in uniform
walking behind me. They were great. They took me down
to a basement of one of the burnt-out houses. When the
raid was over, two of them insisted on taking me to West
Kensington station, made sure the trains were running and
saw me safely onto my train.

It was at that time that the doodlebugs (V1s) started
raining down on London and the home counties. These
were pilotless flying bombs that were directed at London
with just enough fuel to reach their destination. They could
come at any time of day or night.

To everyone's surprise the first V1 was launched one week
after D-Day on 13 June 1944. After D-Day I had started to
think that soon the war would be over.

Up to 9,000 V1s were targeted at southern England,
principally at London. When the pulse jet motor ran out
of fuel it fell out of the sky. They made a distinctive noise
that suddenly stopped when there was no more fuel. I
shall never forget it. If this happened overhead you knew
you were safe and it would land in North London. But if
the motor stopped short of where you were, you started
praying. Its short stubby wings would not allow it to glide,
and it was only its momentum that allowed it to travel a

further small distance before falling to earth and exploding.

At school we were told to get under our desks, but this would have provided little protection. I remember one V1 fell at the junction of Earls Court Road and Kensington High Street in west London, causing complete devastation.

Over 50 per cent of V1s were dealt with before reaching their target. They were shot down by ground-based anti-aircraft guns and by the latest and fastest version of Spitfires and Mosquitoes. These fighters could not get too close to shoot them down as they could be caught by the ensuing blast from one ton of high explosive. They were, however, successful at tipping; flying alongside and tipping the intruder's wings with their own wings so that the V1 flew into the ground before reaching its intended target.

The doodlebugs were followed by the V2 rockets. These were von Braun's rockets, which later formed the basis for the USA's supersonic rockets. The saying was that, if you heard the bang, you were still alive. There was no defence against them. About 1,000 V2s were fired at London, resulting in about 8,000 deaths. They were only dealt with when the Allies took control of the launch sites.

In early 1944 there was a particularly bad assault. During a raid, my mother always woke up me and my brother John and took us into the drawing room. We could hear the planes getting nearer and nearer, and bombs falling. The first one landed in Kensington High Street, destroying the Dorothy Perkins shop. The next few took out private houses along Campden Hill Road. You could hear the explosions getting nearer and nearer.

Opposite our block of flats there was a college for women that was part of London University. The next thing I knew, the college was hit by two bombs and, as the building collapsed with a loud roar, our windows, blackout material and curtains were coming towards us. I did not hear the blast at all, but they always say you do not hear the ones that get you.

We encountered the blast about a second later. John and I, who were sitting on the sofa, were blown over backwards, ending up with the sofa on top of us, which I think saved us. The lights went out momentarily but then came back on. I remember ARP (Air Raid Precautions) wardens shouting, "Put those lights out!" All our curtains and blackout material had gone and there was nothing to stop our lights being seen from outside. My mother got up and quickly turned off our lights.

Left - February 1944; Right - November 2019

The college opposite was housing Maltese refugees in their basement shelters. They rushed out screaming, lighting candles and praying, whereupon the ARP wardens were doing their best at fighting a losing battle to extinguish the candles. By some miracle, no one was killed, though we had now lost our front windows for a fifth time.

The next morning I could not wait to go out to see the damage. The photographs show the building after the bombing and after rebuilding. We had only been about 50 feet from the blast.

In the morning it was business as usual. It was never easy to get to school after an air raid. I usually took the number 9 bus from Kensington High Street. On that morning the road was impassable. There were bomb craters, and flames from a fractured gas main that had ignited, making the High Street impassable.

On a few occasions, one or two students did not turn up for lessons. A little later we would hear that they could not travel to school because bombing made travel impossible. Occasionally, we heard that a pupil had been injured and, on two occasions, that they had been killed.

I remember the temporary bridges built over the Thames river. They were put up rapidly and were capable of taking heavy goods lorries. At the time, Waterloo Bridge was closed as it was considered unsafe, but nothing to do with the war. The temporary bridge near the London County Council building had to take the strain. The bridge was built across the river to Battersea Park.

Waterloo Bridge was replaced with a new bridge, opened in 1944. It was built entirely by women because men were either in the services, or being used to repair bomb damage. Fortunately, none of the temporary bridges were destroyed.

2

LIFE LESSONS

My father was a much better cook that my mother and I was very critical of the food she prepared. This was not fair on my part, as food rationing had severely limited what one could buy during the war. I must have complained once too often. Nanny was told to take me to a British Restaurant, located on the ground floor of an empty house in Campden Hill Road. It was run by the WVS (Women's Voluntary Service, now the Royal Voluntary Service).

British Restaurants had been set up to provide food for people who were really hungry, or who could not afford to eat out in cafes or restaurants. They aimed at providing one third of one's daily food requirement.

I suppose the idea was to teach me to be thankful for what I had at home, but the plan backfired. At the restaurant, we started with brown Windsor soup, then gammon with white sauce, broad beans and chips and finished with spotted dick and custard. There was lemonade or tea to drink. I think the whole meal came to 9d (5p). I thought it was a lovely meal and, when we got home, I asked my mother if we could go again. Clearly I had not been taught a lesson.

My modest tastes in eating out were a contrast to my godfather, who became a Conservative member of Parliament and then a High Court judge. He had been in the Royal Flying Corp in World War One, and had helped to shoot down a Zeppelin. Along with many other people of his age, he was annoyed with the politicians who had made a complete mess of the peace process after that war. He did not serve in World War Two. When in London, he took to dining at the Savoy Hotel. Thanks to my mother, we had rice and eggs throughout the war. She had started buying rice in 1938 at the time of the Munich Crisis and, in fact, her rice stock lasted through to 1947. She also bought a large earthenware crock and filled it with eggs. She then covered the eggs with water glass, a water-soluble form of sodium silicate. This sealed the shells, preventing air from penetrating into the eggs. The occasional one was bad, but the majority survived through to about 1943. You were advised not to boil them, but you could use them for scrambled, fried, or in cooking, due to higher temperatures being used. At the time the food ration provided one egg per person per week.

Food rationing actually became more severe after the war ended, when things like potatoes were rationed for the first time. Sweet rationing continued until the 1950s. After the war, the excellent Minister of Food, Lord Woolton, was replaced by an MP called John Strachey who introduced bread rationing and was not popular.

After the war, we sometimes went as a family to the Trocadero in Piccadilly, mainly to the Salted Almond, their grill room, for lunch or dinner. Due to food rationing we were not allowed to order more than five shillings' (25p) worth of food, which meant you could not order a three-course meal. After about two years this limit was increased to 7s 6d (seven shillings and sixpence, worth 37.5p).

Electricity was also in short supply and I remember there were often power cuts. Street lights were limited to one in four, although many were lit by gas, and buildings were not allowed to leave their lights on after working hours. A hospital on the south coast overcame this problem by buying a surplus submarine and using it to provide electricity to keep the hospital going.

If you travelled from Piccadilly Circus east along Coventry Street, in front of you was Lyons Corner House. The whole building had all its lights on and it was a real landmark. If you looked to the top of the building you would see windmills generating sufficient electricity to power the whole building. That was over 70 years ago and this could teach us something today.

I was sometimes asked whether it had been a problem in wartime having a German surname. One person even asked, rather cheekily, if my father had been the Gauleiter of South Kensington. I do remember an occasion when our surname came under uncomfortable scrutiny. We were on holiday on Jersey, which had really suffered under German occupation, like the rest of the Channel Islands. I was 13 at the time and I had accompanied my father on trip to a local pharmacy to have some films developed.

The woman behind the counter was friendly enough until she asked my father, "What name?" When he said Voelcker, she said, "Is that German?"

"No, it's Dutch," replied my father. "My grandfather settled in Britain from the Netherlands in 1850." The grandfather who had been born in Frankfurt? I was confused.

I said, "But Daddy, you have always told me it was German – why are you kicking my foot?" Perhaps my great-grandfather had anticipated such a situation when he decided to remove the umlaut from our surname after arriving in England.

After five terms at Colet Court, my parents sent me to a boarding preparatory school called Forres. The school was based in Swanage, Dorset, but the buildings had been commandeered by the RAF for the duration of the war. So the school had been relocated to Penn House in Amersham, the home of Lord Curzon. After one term at Penn, the school was able to return to its permanent home in Swanage. Penn House had been a very comfortable place to live, so our return to Swanage was a real shock to the system.

The classrooms were on the ground floor and had radiators, but in the winter there was a great shortage of fuel to heat them. It just so happened that the winter of 1946/7 was the worst in the whole of the 20th century. The bedrooms on the upper floors had no heating at all. We were only allowed to have one blanket and every evening I doubled it over in a futile attempt to keep warm. At lights out, a master would come into the dorm and throw open the windows. One winter's evening I was spotted doubling the blanket and had my bed stripped and told to make it properly. After about 15 minutes, when it was unlikely that he would return, I doubled the blanket once again and closed the nearest window.

Every morning, we had to go for a 20-minute run and afterwards we were dipped like sheep in a plunge pool. If matron thought that we had rushed to get out, we had to go round again and be held under the water for a few seconds. This was followed by breakfast and then by prayers in the chapel. In winter I was so cold that I developed chilblains on my toes. We were told it was all part of character building.

The first form I was placed in did not teach Latin and I complained that I had been learning Latin for over a year at Colet Court. I was then put up a form. This one also did not teach Latin, so I was put up another form. I came top of that form by the end of the first term, which says a lot for the teaching at Colet Court.

Life changed for me in 1947 when on holiday in Looe, Cornwall. I contracted poliomyelitis (otherwise known as polio, then called infantile paralysis) along with about 4,000 people. I was swimming off the main beach with my two brothers when we noticed we were swimming in human excrement. Sewage was piped out to sea by means of a long outfall and was virtually untreated. There was a fracture in the pipe where it passed the main swimming beach. Whether this was due to bomb damage or lack of maintenance I never found out.

Apart from catching polio, the thing I remember most was watching a man on the quayside making ships in Dimple Haig whisky bottles. I was intrigued by the way he placed the boat inside the bottle and how he pulled up the rigging once the boat was inside

My mother had taken all steps to prevent myself and my two brothers from catching the disease. We were not allowed to eat ice creams, go swimming in pools, go to the cinema or other closed places of entertainment. It was just unfortunate that we had chosen one of the worst-hit places in UK for a holiday. This was before the days of the Salk vaccine and polio epidemics were common.

For a while it was touch and go whether I would survive. Then, after a week in a coma, I started to get better. But recovery was slow and I had a whole term off school. My mother had been told by a friend that her daughter had been successfully treated by an osteopath, which was unheard of in those days. He had been trained in the USA and was probably one of the first osteopaths to practice in the UK.

When my mother asked our family doctor to send me to this osteopath, the GP said, "Do you realise that if I send your son to this man, I could be struck off?"

Not to be deterred, my mother contacted the osteopath directly and he agreed to see me. He was great and managed to get movement back into my right leg, which I hadn't been able to use since being ill. I made a pretty good recovery, but I could never run properly afterwards. Unfortunately, the damage done to the nervous system at the time would lead to post-polio syndrome in later years. There's no doubt that having polio had a profound effect on my life. But as much as it left me with physical restrictions, it also strengthened my perseverance and pushed me on to prove myself and exceed people's expectations of me.

In 1949, having passed the common entrance examination to Wellington College in Berkshire, coming top of the entrants for the summer term, I started the next phase of my life.

I did not take to public-school life. The best thing I could say is that I tolerated it. I did not like the idea of fagging, when boys of 13 and 14 had to be servants of house prefects, or being a general fag, when you were forced to do all the dirty jobs no one else wanted to do. Being beaten was a familiar part of life there. One Saturday afternoon I was beaten for not wearing an overcoat while watching a house rugby match. I was well wrapped up and assumed wrongly that I was the best judge of what I needed to wear.

On the sporting side I was not allowed to take part in many activities due to polio. Call me cynical but they weren't protecting me, they simply did not want to be sued if anything went wrong. On many days when teams were being decided, my activity was to go for a walk. I felt like a leper and what made it more painful was that I had made a good recovery from the disease.

There is one occasion I remember well. On 5 February 1952, King George VI died and all lessons were cancelled. In the past the cadet corps of Wellington and Eton had been asked to line the route of the monarch's funeral procession in Windsor. As part of the school's cadet corps, we had 10

My drawing of Wellington

days to train for our part in the ceremony on 15 February, when we would line the Long Walk leading up to the castle.

A number of regular army sergeant-majors were detailed to train us for the event. My section was to be stationed near the entrance to the castle at the top of the Long Walk. We were allocated RSM Brittain for our training. He was reputed to have the loudest voice in the British Army and he certainly knew how to use it. I don't think that any of us had ever been shouted at quite like that before.

"Any questions?" he barked.

"What do I do, sir, if I need spend a penny?"

"You don't," he shouted.

We arrived on site at about 9am and took up our places. I had not had anything to drink since lunch on the previous day for fear of being taken short. We were there for about four hours. My father had told me that on such occasions you should go up on your toes from time to time so that you do not fall or faint.

Fortunately I did not faint, although a few of my compatriots did.

We all had 1917 Lee-Enfield rifles. Most of the time we were at ease, but when the time came, we were at 'rest on your arms reversed'. This meant that the business end of the rifle had to be near your boot, your hands crossed on top of the butt and your head bowed. I do admit to sneaking a few quick looks, having had to wait there for so long.

When the procession arrived, the entrance to the castle being narrower than the Long Walk itself caused a bottle-neck just in front of me. Members of the Royal Family and senior politicians arrived in closed carriages or black cars. The Duke of Edinburgh's head looked out of one of the carriages. "Why has this bloody thing stopped?" he asked. The Duke of Windsor, making a rare visit to the country, walked at the end of the procession, accompanied by the 17-year-old Duke of Kent. I was very relieved when it was all over and we could make our way to the buses to take us back to college.

My school career was mediocre, and I did not achieve anything in the way of prizes or honours. I was happy to leave just before my 17th birthday. My father was having one of his perennial financial crises and the money had run out. Being a compulsive gambler, the horses had not run fast enough. Eighteen months later, my brother John faced a similar fate and had to leave for the same reason. He was in line to become a prefect but was unable to stay long enough to achieve this.

On leaving the college, most students would be headed towards a career in the Army. At the time, the education there was poor and the school was satisfied if it took pupils to the level to pass the Civil Service Examination. This would get them into Sandhurst to become Army officers.

The Master, on addressing school leavers said, "Army is it Voelcker?"

"No, sir."

"You will look back on your school days and think they were the best days of your life," he said.

That's not a good omen for the future, I thought to myself. How right I was. The day I left was the best day of my time there. I felt that Wellington had not done the best for me.

Having passed top of the new arrivals aged 13, I left with nine O levels but no A levels because I was too young to sit the exams. I went home and attended a crammer in Holland Park to get the A levels I needed to go to university.

3

FREEDOM

Having obtained three A level passes in physics, chemistry and mathematics, I applied to join Imperial College, London. At the time, it consisted of three colleges, the Royal College of Science, the City and Guilds College and the Royal School of Mines. Both my father and grandfather had gone to Imperial. My father had obtained a degree in chemistry in 1921 and my grandfather a degree in mining in 1874. So it seemed logical for me to apply to go there, too. However, it was necessary to take an entrance examination, both written and practical, in chemistry. I passed and entered the college in 1954.

I was surprised that my fellow freshers seemed to be much more intelligent than me. At the party for freshers, I met some of the staff who would be teaching us. Professor Levy was the epitome of the absent-minded professor. When asked to tell his story about an absent-minder professor, he said he had forgotten it.

I had never realised how hard one would have to work

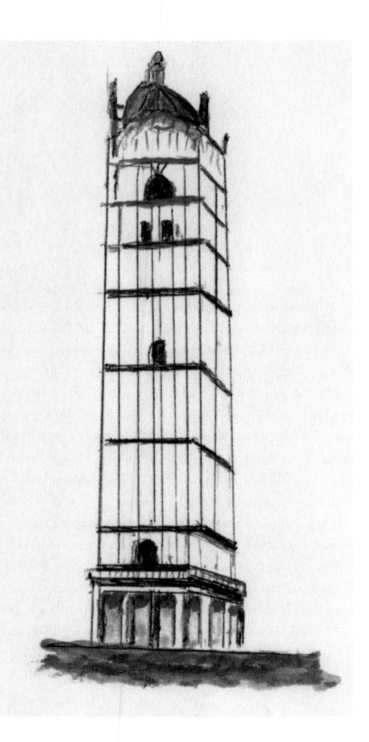

to keep up. I found it necessary to study every Sunday, only having Saturday off. However, my forte was in chemical analysis. I survived the three-year course, obtaining a BSc in chemistry, with ancillary degrees in physics and mathematics.

During my last year I thought I would try to go to Cambridge for a postgraduate course. I decided to apply to Pembroke College because my father had been there before going to Imperial. My father was not keen for me to go to his old college, which I could not understand.

At my interview I was asked whether I had any family members who had been at Pembroke. The tutor asked his secretary to look up Eric Voelcker. She came back, full of apologies, saying that his file was empty, except for his Certificate of Matriculation. This is given as a matter of course to students joining the college and recognises that you are a member of that college for life. My father's career at Pembroke had only lasted five terms, but to his dying day he would not tell me whether he had been rusticated or sent down (suspended or sacked).

The Tutor for Admissions had told me they would accept me if I obtained a second-class degree at Imperial. I was able to tell him that I had obtained a second and was duly admitted in October 1957.

Gaining acceptance into a faculty, in my case Agricultural Science, was not a problem. However, acceptance into a college was not easy due to the sheer number of applicants. Without acceptance you could not join the university, so I was

Pembroke Cambridge

very lucky in being accepted by Pembroke. I was even more lucky to be given a set of two rooms, both a living room and a bedroom, in college. Many of the sets had been split up to provide single rooms to increase in-college accommodation, but mine could not be split up due to its design.

Each room in college was serviced by a 'bedder', a woman who came in daily to clean the room, make the bed and wash up any glasses or crockery. I have never been a beer drinker but took to drinking a South African sherry called Jacaranda. I left a decanter on the side next to the glasses and I noticed the level was going down rather quickly.

I left a note for the culprit saying, 'If you must drink my sherry would you please use a glass, I do not like finding lipstick round the neck of the decanter.' I had heard of other students dealing with the problem by urinating into their decanter. Fortunately, my note quickly did the trick.

My sitting room was often used if we had a few friends in for a drink. The rule at the time was that girls should be out by 10pm, guys out by 11pm and, if you were out, you had to be back in college by midnight. One night, at 11.20pm, we realised that there was still a girl present. We dressed her up in a duffel coat, with the hood over her head and a scarf. I took her down to the college main gate and said, "Goodnight Fred.' There was a grunt from under the duffel coat. Next morning the porter on duty said to me, "Excuse me, sir, but does your friend Fred always wear high-heeled shoes?"

One evening I returned to college after midnight. I could either ring the college bell to be admitted, which would result in being gated (confined to college) for a few days, or climb in over the back gate. I chose the latter. A few nights later, a colleague decided to use the same method of entry. He was mid-climb when, to his horror, he saw the senior tutor coming down the lane. The tutor pulled out his key and swung the gate open, seemingly not noticing the student sitting astride it. He closed the gate and locked it, then walked off. The chap thought he had got away with it. However, after a few yards the tutor turned round, waved and bid my colleague goodnight.

During my post-graduate year I had to wear a long gown, unlike the short ones worn by undergraduates. I had bought this at Ede and Ravenscroft, a shop in Chancery Lane in London. On my first day in residence, the strings of my gown were cut off to show that I was a graduate of a different university.

I received a tremendous feeling of freedom at Cambridge.

Having had polio in 1947 I was not allowed to do anything in the way of sport at my public school. Then at Imperial College there had been little time for anything other than work. But at Cambridge I came into my own. I joined the Pembroke Singers and sang in Handel's Messiah at the Guildhall before Christmas. I became active in politics, taking part in a number of Conservative activities. I took up rowing, taking part in the May Bumps in a scratch crew rowing bow. I was active on Poppy Day when I collected money for charities.

I also made my film debut. Word went round that a film company was going to make a comedy about life in Cambridge and they wanted students to act as extras for the crowd scenes. I volunteered and appeared in some of the scenes. After two days of filming I gave up as it was so boring. The film, called Bachelor of Hearts and starring Hardy Kruger and Sylvia Syms, duly appeared in the cinemas but was not outstanding.

I attended Great Saint Mary's church every Sunday and the midweek talks under the general heading of 'Patterns of Society'. Mervyn Stockwood was the Dean and you had to queue to enter the church as it was so popular. Later, he went on to become Bishop of Southwark.

My best memory of my time at Cambridge was meeting Peter Cook. Peter and I joined Pembroke at the same term in 1957 and we became good friends. He was one of the cleverest, most amusing people I have ever met. He was always writing scripts and submitting them to the BBC. Nearly all were rejected. After his Edinburgh success in Beyond the Fringe, he resubmitted some of the rejected scripts and this time they were snapped up by the BBC.

At Pembroke you were treated like young gentlemen and you were expected to dress and behave like one. You had to wear your gown at dinner in hall, plus a jacket, tie and lace-up shoes. This dress code also applied later when out on the town. The gown had to be in good condition. One evening I was out with Peter and we ran into the Proctor and Bulldogs, the university police. Peter had left over half of his gown on a spike when climbing into college. A Bulldog was dispatched to request Peter to talk to the Proctor for not being properly dressed. When the Proctor requested his name and college, Peter said, "I am the mad vampire," and started flapping the remains of his gown as he ran backwards and forwards. When he was some way away from the Proctor he took to his heels and ran. The Bulldogs, who were picked for their running ability, gave chase but to no avail. The Proctor then turned to me. "I demand to know the name and college of your friend." I said I could not help as I had met him in the pub that evening.

One evening in London, Peter asked me if I would like to see a revue that he had written which was being performed at the Aldwych Theatre. It was good and afterwards I was taken backstage to meet its stars, Fenella Fielding and Kenneth Williams. Fenella said to me, "Darling, who are you?" Kenneth Williams was friendly but rather pleased with himself. I had never realised how short he was.

Then we left the theatre and walked to Soho. On the way we were stopped by a prostitute who asked, "Hello boys, would you like to have some fun?"

Peter replied, 'Good evening, my dear, I do think I have had the pleasure." This was met by a torrent of abuse from the girl.

After Peter's untimely death I was asked by his biographer, Harry Thompson, if I had any stories that he could use. I said I had many, most of which appeared in the book, which was called Peter Cook: A Biography.

After leaving Cambridge I got a job as a consultant in London. For a while, I also found myself spending every spare moment on the Thames. Having enjoyed rowing at Cambridge, I joined the London Rowing Club on the towpath in Putney. You had to train Tuesday, Wednesday and Thursday evening and be out on the water in an eight every Saturday afternoon and Sunday morning. There wasn't much time for socialising away from rowing, so I left after a few months. I had never been so fit.

After having polio in 1947, I was encouraged to rebuild muscles by using weights and it's something I've done all my life. In 1960 I had my first encounter with a gym in London when the first health club in the UK opened in Tottenham Court Road. I joined and went there about twice a week on my way home from work. It contained free weights, machines, saunas and sunbeds. The instructors were well-built, friendly Americans. They had been brought in to get the club going and were replaced after a few months by local staff.

The club was men-only and the clientele were from all walks of life and professions. I recognised a few actors and other well-known people, including the principal actors from the show South Pacific. I met three Rhodesian guys and I told them I was shortly going to live in their country. They were most helpful, telling me that there were some good gyms in main towns such as Salisbury and Bulawayo.

Regular use of the gym was good for my confidence. Being in my early twenties I was able to build muscle and lose my skinny appearance, which had earned me the rather cruel nickname 'Belsen' at school.

On my first visit to the health club I tried using the sauna. I felt very uncomfortable sitting there surrounded by naked guys cheek by jowl, who smiled and winked at me when I entered. When two guys, obviously aroused, moved to sit next to each other, I decided not to linger. Next time I decided to use a sunbed instead.

4

SOUTHERN AFRICA

Always keen to travel and see the world, I decided to emigrate to southern Africa and take advantage of the job opportunities out there. I flew out to Rhodesia in 1962 and stayed for nearly six years. I started job hunting as soon as I got there, but I never seemed to land the jobs I really wanted. I then met a man who was ex-Royal Navy and now CEO of an engineering firm producing metal alloys for the motor industry. He looked at my CV and said, "You will never get a job with this, you are over-qualified. Let me write one for you." I was astonished when I saw it. He had allowed me 5 GCEs only and no university degrees. It did the trick. Within 24 hours I had a job with British American Tobacco in Salisbury on a salary of £70 per month (about £850 in 2020).

This was not Salisbury in Wiltshire, but the capital city of Southern Rhodesia. After six months of working for the tobacco company, I decided to look for a better job. I contacted the Metal Box Company of Central Africa Ltd, part of a worldwide packaging group with headquarters in London. It had two factories in Rhodesia, one in Salisbury and the other in Bulawayo. I was taken on as a management trainee at a salary of £85 per month (about £1,050 in 2020). I stayed with the company for five years, ending up in charge of the Bulawayo operation and number three in the company, which employed about 500 people.

Salisbury, now known as Harare, is a lovely, well-designed city with jacaranda trees everywhere and many fine buildings. On Friday evenings some of us would go for a drink at Le Coq D'Or, a night spot in the centre of the city. It was very popular with South Africans who flew in for a weekend to enjoy things that weren't allowed in their own country. It provided food and drink, a band for dancing and a cabaret.

One evening the performer was Pamela the Tantalising Tassel Tosser. Apart from a few sequins, she had four tassels, two on her breasts and another two on her behind. The highlight of her act was to get all four going at the same time, which, considering the extra weight she carried, did not seem to me to be very difficult. Suddenly there was a roll on the drums, the lights went out and ultra-violet lights illuminated her tassels. "Now we come to the hard bit," she announced.

A rather drunk member at the bar replied, "I have it waiting for you over here, darling." This brought about much applause from the audience.

On another such evening the cabaret was provided by Miss Fluffles. Unlike Pamela, she was lean and slightly muscular. To me, her act was much more of an art form than her predecessor. I was so intrigued that I took her out to dinner at Meikles Hotel. It turned out to be one of the most disappointing evenings I had ever had. She made it quite plain that she was not interested in men. "So don't have any expectations," she warned. "I despise the lot of you." She told me she was a lesbian and her only love was her manager. "I could not do this job if I did not hate you all."

After that conversation killer, the only thing I could think to say was, "How do you get them to stick on?"

"Trade secret," came her reply. It was a great relief when it was time for me to take her back for her second show.

The History

As a visitor in southern Africa, it's good to know something of its complicated past. In 1923 Southern Rhodesia was asked if they would like to join South Africa or govern themselves. They voted two to one for the latter. Then, in 1953, it became part of the Federation of Rhodesia and Nyasaland, along with Northern Rhodesia and Nyasaland. Each of the three territories was responsible for their own internal government. However, the Federal Government was responsible for things affecting all three countries: finance, transport, immigration, posts and telegraphs, police and defence. The Federation got off to a good start and became the fastest-developing part of the world.

Salisbury was the capital city of Southern Rhodesia with a Governor based in Government Lodge. It was also the capital of the Federation with a Governor-General based in Government House.

Many Europeans and South Africans were attracted to the country, bringing with them their families, their skills, their professions and their money. The Kariba Dam was built across the Zambezi River linking Southern and Northern Rhodesia. This was the second link between the two countries, the first being the Victoria Falls Bridge. This was part of Cecil Rhodes' plan to build a rail link from Cape Town to Cairo in Egypt.

Many industries were set up, many being subsidiaries of established overseas companies. These included firms in engineering, electronics, packaging, foodstuffs, pharmaceuticals, printing, mining, construction, tobacco-related products and tourism. Southern Rhodesia, with its tremendous income from tobacco sales, provided finance for the poorer part of the Federation, relieving the UK of having to do it.

Then the British Government decided to dissolve the Federation and it ended in late 1963. Northern Rhodesia and Nyasaland were told they could have full independence nine months later. Northern Rhodesia became Zambia and Nyasaland became Malawi.

Victoria Falls bridge

Main falls

Southern Rhodesia, on the other hand, was denied full independence. It had been told at the outset that if the Federation did not work, it would have immediate full independence on its dissolution. But now it was told it was not ready for it, despite the fact that it had been self-governing since 1923 and had achieved great economic success.

A general election was called and was won by the Rhodesian Front (RF), led initially by Winston Field and later by Ian Smith. Party members of RF did not consider that Field, who was born and brought up in the UK, was trying hard enough in pressing the UK for full independence. He was replaced by Ian Smith, who was Rhodesian born and bred, and fought for the UK in World War Two as a pilot in the RAF. He was shot down over Italy, taken prisoner, escaped and joined the partisans fighting with resistance groups.

Attitudes amongst the white population were hardening. They were incensed that, having run a very successful country for over 40 years, and having raised living standards to the second highest in Africa, they were now being denied full independence. As a result, African advancement, which had progressed well under the Federal Government, was halted.

I knew someone in London who worked for the Foreign Office. He visited Southern Rhodesia on a two-week fact-finding mission. I saw him again when I was on holiday in

London. I asked him how he got on with the Council of Chiefs, the body representing Africans. He did not know what I was talking about. He clearly had not heard of them, nor had he talked to them. Here was a man whose job was to help decide the future of a country of six million people and he had not bothered to gather all the necessary facts.

I got the impression that the UK Government had already decided what to do and then tried to justify it with visits by civil servants on rather bogus 'fact-finding visits'. It was rumoured that the UK Government was afraid that if they granted Southern Rhodesia full independence, this would affect the UK's exports to member countries of the Organisation of African Unity.

One of the problems was intimidation in the black townships. People were afraid to go out after dark due to demands for money, and threats and beatings by thugs from the two main black groups. For a brief time I joined the Central Africa Party, set up to ensure that when the country had a black government, it would be safe for all races to live and work in harmony.

At the time of an election, the Central Africa Party's chairman, Samson Zarwi, went round the townships on a bicycle, ringing a hand bell and telling people to vote. The Central Africa Party received two votes in the election: those of the party leader and his wife.

Samson was warned by the Nationalists to stop or he would be in trouble.

He refused. His house was burnt down and although his wife and children escaped, Samson was very badly burned. I visited him in hospital. He had a white streak down his body where his flesh had been burnt off and he was unable to work. He was too disabled to ever work again.

At that time, the voters' roll consisted of 15 per cent African and other non-European people, a number that was growing at a satisfactory rate. On becoming prime minister, Ian Smith put about 300 known troublemakers under house arrest in the Low Veld, the southern part of the country. Mugabe and Nkomo were two of those detained.

Mugabe was leader of the predominantly Shona tribe, whilst Nkomo was leader of the Matabeles in the western part of the county. The two could not get on at all. Mugabe had affiliations with China, whilst Nkomo had links with Russia. This act of house arrest received tremendous support in the African townships. People could go out without fear of intimidation, and cinemas and beer halls were full once again. A number of African workers in the factory said, 'Ian Smith very good man.'

Eastern Catarat

Devil's Catarat

Dr. Livingstone

Rhodesia's Finest Hour

On 11 November 1965 the Smith Government took independence unilaterally (UDI), since they felt cheated by Britain for not being granted the full independence they'd been promised at the end of the Federation. Immediately, the United Nations (UN) put sanctions on all member states, forbidding them from trading with Southern Rhodesia. However, at that time Germany was not a member of the UN. France took the view that they were not going to be told by anybody whom they could trade with and continued trading. In actual fact you could buy anything you liked, mainly through Romania, if you had hard currency (sterling, dollars, francs etc). Apart from banning all trade with Rhodesia, the UK Government banned Rhodesian currency from being legal tender.

Following the UDI decision, Prime Minister Harold Wilson sent RAF Lightning fighters to Lusaka, Zambia's capital, as a show of force. The RRAF (Royal Rhodesian Air Force), was well-equipped with Hawker Hunter fighters, Canberra bombers, Alhouette helicopters, Dakotas and even some old Vampire fighters.

The RRAF wanted to buy Westland helicopters, but Westland said their planes were not suitable to operate at the required altitude. The air was too thin. They then bought Alouette helicopters from France, who were not worried about the altitude. A Rhodesian friend commissioned in the

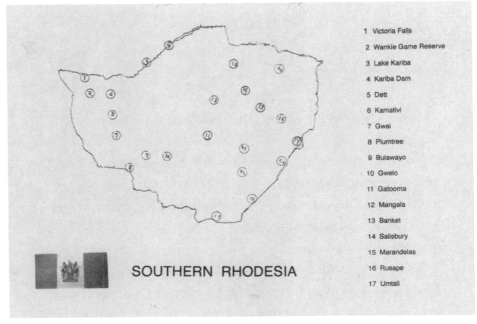

1 Victoria Falls
2 Wankie Game Reserve
3 Lake Kariba
4 Kariba Dam
5 Dett
6 Kamativi
7 Gwai
8 Plumtree
9 Bulawayo
10 Gwelo
11 Gatooma
12 Mangala
13 Banket
14 Salisbury
15 Marandelas
16 Rusape
17 Umtali

SOUTHERN RHODESIA

Map of Southern Rhodesia

Smith signing

army lost his life, along with others, in Alhouette crashes due to altitudes problems.

Air traffic control for the area was based in the Rhodesian capital Salisbury. So RAF planes had to ask permission from the other side to take off. Some of the RRAF pilots had transferred from the RAF, so many knew one another. Pilots from both nations had great fun in flying together in formation down the Zambezi River, to the annoyance of both Zambian and British politicians.

By the time UDI was declared, I had progressed within the Metal Box Company and was now running their Bulawayo factory. One line produced open-top cans for food products and motor oil, while the second line produced rectangular cans for corned beef. Both lines produced five cans every second.

The day after UDI was declared, the African on reception called me in to say that there was a Mr Ushima who was asking to see me. He was the representative of Mitsui of Japan, based in Johannesburg, a firm that produced tinplate. He had come to tell me that, if the Steel Company of Wales (SCOW) were not able to supply us with tinplate, Mitsui would be happy to do so. To keep us going they would airfreight the first order to us but after that they would supply us by sea.

UDI brought about some strange situations. I was in the UK for Christmas 1965, six weeks after independence. The UK press were saying that Central African Airways

THE METAL BOX COMPANY OF CENTRAL AFRICA LIMITED

BULAWAYO BRANCH NOTICE No. 3/65

Date of Issue : 11th November . 1965

The Prime minister will speak to the Nation at 1.15 pm. today. Everyone should return work after lunch in the normal way. Radios will be provided in the factory so that everyone may hear his statement.

Umnuzuna u Prime Minister uzakuluma emoyeni ekuluma lesizwe namuhla emini ngo 1.15 pm. Wonke umuntu kufanele abuyele emsebenzini ngemuva. kokudia njengansukuzonke. Ama radios azabekona e factory ukaze wonke umuntu azizwele udaba lwake.

R.M. Voelcker

R.M.VOELCKER
BRANCH MANAGER

The Notice I put up in the Factory

The notice I put up in the factory on Independence Day

Vikers Viscount

(CAA), the Rhodesian airline, only had enough fuel to continue operations until the first week of January. I was returning to Salisbury by South African Airways and then on to Bulawayo by CAA around 20 January. After UDI, the Rhodesian part of CAA changed its name to Air Rhodesia. The planes had to be parked the correct way round as the other side said Zambia Airways.

I assumed that I would have to travel from Salisbury to Bulawayo by train. When I arrived at Salisbury airport, I was told that a flight to Bulawayo was leaving in 40 minutes. I assumed that CAA must have more fuel than the UK thought. In fact, petrol, diesel and aviation fuel were being supplied from Durban in South Africa.

In Rhodesia there were five oil companies – BP, Shell, Mobil, Total and Caltex – providing fuel for motor vehicles.

These were commandeered by the Rhodesian Government and put into a new organisation called GENTA to pool their resources. They appointed BP to run it, which they did very well. At the time BP had not been fully privatised and was partly owned by the British Government. Fuels were brought in by rail from their refinery in Durban. South African subsidiaries of UK firms were not included in the boycott and hence British firms could circumnavigate sanctions legally by supplying goods through these subsidiaries.

This was a period of change and growth for newly independent Rhodesia. The building of Lake Kyle dam near Fort Victoria had provided the Low Veld with sufficient water to develop the area for farming. When tobacco sales shrunk, the Low Veld area was further developed and a profitable secondary industry emerged – sugar. Two crops of sugar cane per year were now possible, resulting in high-quality sugar, one of the cheapest in the world. The Low Veld area and some of the tobacco-growing areas went over to successfully growing cereals. The country became the bread basket of southern Africa.

The clothing industry in Bulawayo expanded rapidly and new industries were set up. These included the manufacture of fridges and freezers, postage stamps, vehicle rebuilding. Many existing factories increased their size to cope with increased local demand for radios, textiles, shoes, household products and pharmaceutical products. At the same time, new restaurants and hotel extensions were set up to cope with the large increase of tourists to the country. They came from the USA, Germany, France, South Africa and the UK. A plentiful supply of hard currency came into the country.

5

A BRIT ABROAD

was fearful that, after UDI, our customers would lose out on sales and hence would require fewer cans. I was also worried about my position: a British subject, working in a country that was in insurrection towards the Crown. Was this treason? I asked the Metal Box head office in London to clarify my position. They wrote back saying I was doing a grand job so stick at it. I replied that if they did not obtain clarity on my position by the end of the month, they could take this letter as my resignation. They quickly replied that they had obtained a ruling from the Foreign Office that it was alright to continue at my job. I asked for this in writing, which I eventually received.

I saw a potential customer for our corned beef cans in Botswana. When I visited the cannery in Lobatse, I received great interest in buying from us. I took with me some dummy cans. The only difference was that ours carried a small company imprint of MBCA, whilst the ones from Johannesburg had MB4. Our cans were also cheaper than the ones they were currently buying. Since we were operating a single shift for Rhodesian customers, it was simple to lay on a second shift for Botswana using Mitsui's tinplate.

There were problems to overcome. The goods must not be traceable to a Rhodesian supplier. I found a firm in South Africa who were quite happy, for a fee, to supply new documentation stating 'Produce of South Africa'. They stressed, however, that the goods must not show any trace of their true identity. First of all, the goods must be sent down the railway line in South African Railways (SAR) trucks and locomotives, not Rhodesian Railways (RR) trucks. The same applied to the cardboard cartons in which the empty cans would be packed. They currently stated, 'Proudly made in Rhodesia', so this had to go, as did our MBCA imprint. There must be nothing to indicate country of origin.

Once all that was agreed, we were now ready to start manufacturing for our new customer. I am glad to say all went well. We were then approached by a cannery at Damara in South West Africa (now Namibia) to repeat the exercise. This time it was easier, having done it before.

Every other day I had to contact the South African Ministry of Transport in Pretoria to arrange the supply of SAR trucks and steam locomotives. Sometimes I spoke directly to Ben Schoeman the South African transport minister. Although I never met him, we became quite friendly over the telephone.

We were now making substantial profits through recovery of fixed assets and, for our size, we became the most profitable factory in the group. I needed to recruit someone to be in charge of raw material quality and finished product. I took on a young African who had just returned from London University with a good degree in mathematics and statistics – just what I wanted.

On his first morning, things initially went well. However, some time later the African staff downed tools and refused to work. I could not understand what was wrong. It turned out that I had recruited a Mashona to work in a factory staffed by Matabele. The two tribes hated each other. I telephoned my managing director in Salisbury for advice. He said, "No problem, sack him."

I gave him three months' salary and suggested that he looked for work in Mashonaland, the eastern part of the country. He said how sorry he was, explaining that after four years in UK, getting used to European ways, he forgot there could be such problems on his return home.

During my four-year stint of running the Bulawayo factory, I was amazed by some of the policies in place for the staff. Senior staff consisted of 'Whites' who had just been taken on, or had been with the company for some time. They got four weeks' holiday per year, private medical insurance and paid leave to visit Cape Town every other year. It was wrongly thought that it was necessary for Whites to return to sea level every other year for the benefit of their health.

Junior staff consisted of Africans who had responsible jobs but were treated differently. They got two weeks' holiday a year, with no medical aid insurance or trips to Cape Town.

I had to sack two Whites who were fine in the morning but weren't often sober after lunch. I argued with the Board that it was quite wrong to have this distinction between the Whites and Africans. We should have one category of staff whose remuneration and benefits were based on the job and not on race. This was eventually agreed.

I promoted four Africans to the senior staff with all the improved conditions. The only problem I encountered from one of the four was whether the medical aid scheme would pay for witch doctors' fees? The answer was no. Two of the four were a great success and two let me down.

I was told by some of the Afrikaners – white people of European heritage – in the factory that they could have told me that the scheme would fail. However, in my view, a 50 per cent rate first-time round was a success.

Afrikaans is the principal language of Afrikaners and those of mixed race, known as Coloureds. It is based on Dutch with some German, English and African dialects. Pure Dutch is known as High Dutch, whilst Afrikaans is referred to as Dutch.

We had plenty of spare land on the factory site and myself and Colin Bungay, my second in command, designed and made a tennis court. We tried to teach some of the staff how to play. However, most of the time was spent retrieving tennis balls from the factory's railway siding.

I was asked by the South African Metal Box Company

if I would be interested in being considered for the post of manager of the company's plastics factory at Isando near Johannesburg airport. Whilst this would have been a good step up, I did not want to spend my life in South Africa under apartheid. I therefore refused.

I eventually decided, with much regret, to return home to the UK. I could not see any long-term future for the white man in that part of the world. I borrowed a friend's substantial house in Bulawayo to hold a farewell party. I made it a black-tie affair, got caterers to lay on the food and an African band to provide the music. My managing director came down from Salisbury for it. His wife was away in Johannesburg, so he was determined to enjoy himself.

One of my female guests decided to sit on a glass-topped dining room table. There was the sound of breaking glass as she fell through, landing on the floor amongst broken glass. Fortunately she was in a relaxed state, through ample supply of wine, and completely unhurt.

Once the party was well underway, the MD announced that the company would pay for the party, including repair to the glass table. That was all very well but I was trying to use up the money I was not allowed to take out of the country.

I told my houseboy, Robert, that I was going back to England but that I would find him a suitable position, which I did. He was very upset and said he wanted to come with me. I said he would not like it because of the weather and, in any case, what would he do without his many umfazies (girlfriends)? He said he would have to find some new umfazies in England.

He then asked me who would look after master? Who would make his bed, clean master's house, clean his shoes, do master's washing and cook his meals? I said that I would have to do it all myself. Robert thought for a while and then said, "England is no place for a white man." I think he may have had a point.

Robert met my younger brother, John, who stayed with me for a month on his way to Australia. Robert said to me, "I like boss John, he looks just like Harold Wilson." This remark did not go down well with my brother.

I decided to give a party for all employees which, in practice, was largely the African staff. Fortunately it was a great success. It all got emotional and I believe they were sorry that I was going. One of my promoted four suggested something in Matabele, which I did not understand. He was suggesting that a traditional dance be performed, which usually only happened for a departing chief. One African said to me that he had never known this honour being bestowed upon a white man.

I left feeling I had done a good job under difficult conditions and was now much more confident in myself. I had also learned much about industry and management and had run a successful enterprise under difficult conditions.

My decision to leave was not easy, but in retrospect it proved to be the right one. It equipped me well for my next move.

Once I was back in the UK and had found a job, I received a call from the Inland Revenue asking me how much I had earned in Rhodesia from 6 April in that tax year to the date I started working in UK. I told them I had not earned any money at all.

The Inland Revenue inspector said they knew I had been working for the Metal Box Company in Bulawayo and must have earned something. 'What did you live on?" they asked. I said I was paid in worthless pieces of paper. I pointed out that the British Government had declared the Rhodesian currency was no longer legal tender. Hence, in British eyes, my Rhodesian income was nil. I was told they would have to get a ruling from the Bank of England. A few days later I received a call back. According to the Bank of England I was correct in my argument.

Postscript

In view of what has happened since I left Rhodesia in 1967, I find it very sad the way its people have suffered.

First of all, there was a civil war. The Rhodesian Army, manned mainly by African soldiers, was gaining the upper hand. The saying was, it consisted of white officers with black privates.

However, the South African President Vorster wanted a benign black state to the north to protect their northern border. The only way he could achieve this was to stop supplying Rhodesia with arms, fuel and ammunition. You cannot fight a war without these.

In 1979 the Lancaster House Conference was held to decide on the country's future and Black Rule. In my day, there were a growing number of Africans and other non-whites on the voters' roll, and it was estimated that parity would be reached in nine years. That would have been by 1977, two years earlier than the Lancaster House Agreement. Instead, the people got a government under Mugabe and his fellow villains. Between them they broke the country financially, killed numerous Matabeles and forced most of the Whites and Indians to leave. The Rev Canaan Banana became president of the new republic for a short time. He was a figure of ridicule, later a figure of disgrace, and the country became known as the Banana Republic.

Nearly all the tobacco farms were seized without any compensation. These were given to Mugabe's cronies as weekend retreats, with no intention of producing saleable crops or providing employment. Many jobs were lost, forcing people to find work in other countries, causing problems with indigenous people. The main source of income for the country were the postal orders sent home from workers forced to work abroad to keep their families alive.

A great country was destroyed by a bunch of ruthless thugs, driven only by their own greed and lust for power, who did not care about the country or its inhabitants.

6

ALWAYS REVERSE BEFORE
GOING FORWARD

On my return from Africa in 1967, I applied to the four top UK firms of management consultants based in London. It was a good moment to be recruited into the business. At the time, Barbara Castle was Minister of Labour and there had been a plague of labour disputes over workers' pay. So a law was passed stating that people could only have a pay increase if they could show a percentage increase in productivity greater than the increase in pay being demanded. In practice, this meant that independent consultants would have to be used to study working practices and identify where improvements could be made. Firms could not do it for themselves. For this reason there was a great increase in demand for management consultants' services.

Two of the big four firms invited me to come for a first and then a second interview. My preferred firm, P-E Consulting Group Ltd, then asked me to attend an all-day group interview along with nine other applicants. Fortunately, a friend who had already joined the company described the form it would take.

He said it would start with a discussion on a current problem facing the country. In my case the subject was, 'In View of the Current Wave of Strikes in the Country, Strikes Should be Banned by Law'. My friend had advised me not to be the first person to talk, but to come in second and, if possible, shoot the first one down.

The first speaker said that the country was being crippled by strikes and hence they should be banned by law. I had to think on my feet. Coming in second, I pointed out that I had recently worked in southern Africa, where strikes had been banned to little effect. I explained how two million African gold miners had gone on strike for more pay and better conditions, leaving the government powerless to do anything about it. The strike had led ultimately to negotiation and a deal being reached.

After the morning session, we had a good lunch with most kinds of drink

being provided. But I followed my friend's advice and I chose soft drinks only.

A week later I received a letter offering me a job, which I accepted. Training started a month later, in October 1967, for the eight of us who had been selected. We could not be used on fee-paying work until we had been trained. This consisted of six weeks at the training centre and two four-week periods assisting established consultants with their assignments.

At the end of the first training session we were asked which part of the country we would like to work in. I said I would like to work in the London area, or in the home counties. So they sent me to Greenock in Scotland. We had with us a consultant called Rolf from the German branch of the firm who wanted to improve his English. So he was sent to Glasgow.

On the last day of the initial training session we were told that there were some nice assignments, but there was one that was going horribly wrong. Our supervisor said he felt sorry for the poor trainee who was being sent there. It turned out to be me.

The client was Greenock Corporation. My role was to study the joinery section that made replacement doors and windows, and also carried out general repairs for council houses and flats. The manager, Ebenezer, was supposed to run the shop but had given up managing a few years ago. His problem seemed to be alcohol related. In the meantime, Willie the shop steward had taken it upon himself to act as manager.

However, with my arrival, Ebenezer thought it was a good moment to show he was the real manager, so he told me where I should start. On the first morning I went out with a joiner whose job was to repair sash cords in windows. We got to the first address and when the joiner pressed the doorbell, there was no reply. He tried again but still no reply. "I know she is in," he said. He knelt down and called through the letterbox, "Hello hen, I am not the rent man." The door was then opened and we went in.

The resident seemed to know the joiner and she disappeared to make tea. "I see you have brought a friend with you," she said, referring to me. There were two small children running around. "I am looking after the wee wains today," she explained. "These are my grandchildren."

After tea, the joiner found a newspaper to read, then more tea. Then, finally, he looked at the broken sash cord. "This is not straightforward. It will take too long, so I will have to come back another day," was his verdict. We returned to the joinery shop after a wasted morning and no work done.

Looking at a book of standard times for replacing sash cords, I discovered that it should take 15 minutes at a rating of 100 – a rating of 100 is the equivalent of someone, properly motivated, walking at 4 mph. 'Properly motivated' seemed to be the key phrase. I thought to myself, Is this really what being a management consultant means? I had looked on myself as being God's gift to UK management. I hadn't envisaged sash windows and tea drinking.

At the end of the first day I went to my car to drive to the Tontine Hotel where I was staying. As I drove forward I realised I had a puncture in both front tyres, caused by the nails that had been balanced underneath them. I was told next day that you should always reverse before going forward, to let any nails fall away. Even better, you should not park in the same place every day, but still make sure to reverse before driving off.

The next day, Ebenezer decided that I should look at a young man making a new sash window. Before starting, I asked the young man if he minded me watching him. He didn't. After about 30 minutes, shop steward Willie told everyone to stop working. "The consultant is studying an apprentice, which is against union rules." He then called a strike. I think Willie had looked upon this as an opportunity to regain his position of self-appointed acting manager. But I thought to myself, This is the end of my career as a consultant.

I had moved out of the Tontine Hotel and booked into a cheaper one further down the estuary. I was feeling very low after the events of the day, so went into the bar to have a stiff drink. To my astonishment, there behind the bar was Willie the shop steward. Dressed in a mess jacket and bow tie, he was clearly moonlighting. Willie looked surprised to see me. "What are you doing here?" he asked. I told him I had just booked in. I asked him whether he would like a drink. He said, "I do not drink with the likes of you."

The next evening when I went in to the bar, I caught Willie decanting whisky from a brand I had not heard of into bottles labelled Johnny Walker, Grouse, Bell's, Haig and other famous brands. He said that at least half of the whisky he sold had to be the anonymous brand, which turned out to be owned by the brewery. I helped him by holding the funnel as he poured. After that we were buddies.

Later that evening a couple came in. The man ordered two Bell's whiskies. In an obvious attempt to impress, he turned to his partner and said, 'I can always tell the difference.' I looked at Willie and smiled. A little later Willie said, "Forget the strike they will all be back at work in the morning."

The low productivity within Greenock was clearly caused by a complete lack of management. I thought matters could be helped if the corporation were buying doors, windows and so on from builders suppliers.

Two weeks later, Greenock was hit by a freak storm which caused much damage. All regular work stopped and operatives were put on repair work.

I was then told to look at the work being done by electricians rewiring council houses. This was a welcome break for me as it meant I was working indoors with people of much higher intelligence. I was impressed by the way they organised and carried out their work.

At the end of this training assignment, I left feeling that my input into a very troubled situation was of little use. The lack of supervision in the joiner's shop had allowed the workforce to do exactly what they liked, and hence productivity was extremely low. I heard later that the Corporation had closed the Building and Maintenance section. They had decided to buy windows, doors and so on from an outside supplier. So I had at least been correct in my assessment of the situation.

The staff manager said on my return to London that I had survived a difficult assignment in Greenock. I was now ready for my first fee-earning assignment. He wanted me to carry out a similar job but in Glasgow Corporation, which was roughly ten times the size of Greenock. Once again, the purpose was to increase productivity of direct labour in order to receive a pay increase.

The Building Works Department employed 7,000 people in all aspects of construction and through to repairs and demolition. Their offices were located just off George Square. My job was to study the work of drivers in the section.

Each foreman was provided with a van and a driver. However, this proved unnecessary, as all foremen drove themselves to work in their own cars. Removal of the drivers and financial compensation for use of the foremen's own cars resulted in an immediate jump in the section's productivity and was very popular with the foremen. The redundant drivers were found work elsewhere in the Corporation.

One problem solved, I travelled with some of the lorry drivers to find out what was involved in their work. They seemed to work well, but deliveries were required all over the city in an unplanned way. Helping to improve forward planning of routes saved both time and money.

We had a rule in our consulting practice that, when having meetings with union representatives, there should always be a second consultant present to take notes. There had been instances in the past where only one consultant had been present, and a union representative had announced to its members that agreement had been reached on items that had not even been discussed.

My German colleague, Rolf, was working with scaffolders to make them more productive. He had been in the Hitler Youth and it had left its mark.

He drove a very hard bargain.

At the end of the meeting the convenor thanked Rolf and said his English was not at all bad. Then he turned to me and said, "But Mr Voelcker's English is excellent," thinking that I, too, was German.

I said, "Ja danke, danke."

When we left the meeting Rolf said, "I think we won the argument."

My assignment was proving to be difficult because I was not getting the cooperation of management. They resented that consultants had been called in to sort out and raise productivity in sections under their control.

I was told by the union involved that a meeting was being held on Sunday evening and they would be grateful if I would attend. The union concerned was the Transport and General Workers.

I went in, dressed casually, to find them all in their Sunday best. I was greeted with a chorus of boos and catcalls, followed by renditions of 'Why was he born so beautiful?' I raised both arms in the air and said, "Thanks fans.'

After the meeting had dealt with union affairs, I was asked to tell them about my work and how it was proceeding. I told them that I was meeting resentment from those who thought it unnecessary to call in consultants. It was felt by management that they did not like outside interference in their sections. They were totally missing the point that outside consultants were needed in order to introduce and implement ways of increasing productivity so that salaries could be increased. Legally they could not do it for themselves. The union members showed great interest in what I said and some useful suggestions were made.

To my surprise, it was proposed that they should hold a one-day strike in support of me and to aid progress. I thanked them for the offer, which would have meant them losing a day's pay. I said I could not accept as it was management paying my bill. If a strike were to go ahead, I told them, I would be removed from the assignment. I said how much I appreciated the offer and thanked them very much.

During my time in Clydeside I often flew home for the weekend. On one such weekend I went to Glasgow Airport, only to be told my flight had been cancelled due to strike action. Also at the airport was the senior consultant who supervised my assignment and I explained my predicament. He said, "Leave it to me." He found the trade union convenor and told him that he had ruined my weekend.

The convenor then went and arranged to block the next flight instead. So I had my weekend home after all.

Knowing no one in Glasgow, I joined the Conservative Party and became a member of the Conservative Political Centre (CPC). Every month the party headquarters in London asked every constituency to debate the same topic on a current issue. The minutes of the meeting were sent back to London as a means of taking the political temperature across the country.

It was the time that Enoch Powell had made his 'Rivers of Blood' speech. Earlier at a by-election in Smethwick, the Conservatives won the seat in a Labour stronghold using a racist slogan.

The question for debate was to test the feeling of the meeting about the flood of immigrants coming into the country. The general feeling was it was a good thing as long as they came in a controlled way and we were not swamped.

One team member, in summing up, said, "I have nothing against the darkies, it's those Pakie Bastards I cannot stand." I do not think he realised why we were all laughing.

Another fellow consultant was working with the demolition gang pulling down some of the Victorian 'closes', which were flats with shared kitchens, baths and toilet facilities on each landing. The purpose was to study the methods employed and to improve productivity. It was found that this could be achieved by slightly altering the working procedures.

On the first day of the new scheme a wall fell the wrong way and demolished some parked cars, which fortunately were not occupied. The union was quick to ensure that this episode was not due to a fault in the scheme. All the members liked the new scheme and did not want it withdrawn or changed.

The work that I and my colleagues carried out went well and the workforce easily earned a pay increase since their productivity had risen sufficiently. Unlike my first assignment, I left this one feeling I had done a decent job.

7

SHIPBUILDING

I n 1968 I was asked by the staff manager of my consultancy what my religion was. I said it was Church of England. He said that was alright because if I had said Catholic, I would not have been able to work on my next assignment. I could not imagine where I could be going. It turned out to be Belfast in Northern Ireland.

Knowing nothing about the politics of that part of the world, I did not understand why he had asked that question. The assignment was in Harland and Wolff's shipyard. Once I started work there, however, it soon became clear that Harland and Wolff and their sister company, Short Brothers and Harland, would not employ Catholics.

Harland and Wolff dated from 1861 and was formed by Edward James Harland and Gustav Wilhelm Wolff. It is perhaps most famous for being the shipyard that built the Titanic. It also built many other well-known ships, including Titanic's sister ships Britannic and Olympic for the White Star Line, and many for the Royal Mail Lines, P&O, Shaw

Savill and Union Castle Lines. The last passenger liner built there was the Canberra in the mid 1960s. They also made an important contribution during World War Two, building aircraft carrier HMS Formidable in 1940, as well as many warships including HMS Belfast, now moored in the River Thames. Their sister company, Short Brothers and Harland, built the famous Short Sunderland flying boats for Coastal Command, which gained an excellent record in sinking German submarines.

The Belfast assignment turned out to be one of the best I'd encountered. I have always been interested in ships of all sizes, so this was perfect for me. I worked as part of a team of six consultants employed to help to reduce the

HMS Formidable

firm's losses. When the firm had become bankrupt, the UK Government had agreed to bail them out as long as they employed consultants.

They were also told that they must construct a building dock capable of building much larger ships, such as super-tankers and bulk carriers. The building dock was being constructed by Wimpey. When I arrived, I was told that Wimpey stood for 'We Import More Paddies Each Year'.

The shipyard had received an order for their first very large crude oil carrier (VLCC) tanker. It would be the largest to be built in Europe. Because of their size, these ships should be constructed in a dry dock and floated out by flooding the dock. The traditional way was to build a ship on a slip and then to launch it stern-first into the water.

Despite being warned by others in the industry not to build a ship of that size on a slip, the decision was taken to start work immediately, rather than wait for the building dock to be completed. Without a building dock they should have built it in two halves and joined it together afloat. However H and W knew better.

The ship was launched in the conventional way, down a slip. On hitting the water, the ship slewed, breaking its back and taking a crane with it. When I arrived, the VLCC was docked whilst people were trying to work on a way to straighten it out. In the end they had to cut it in half, remove the damaged section, replace it and then join it together afloat.

My job was to work in the preparation shop where steel plates were cut into shapes for ships under construction. The first step was for a joiner to construct a wooden template of the required shape. Then people drew round the templates with chalk on to the steel. Other people then cut round the chalk lines with hand burners to obtain the steel components.

In all, these operations took eight to ten people. In Germany, however, these jobs were done by just one person. A man in an office would have a one-tenth scale drawing in front of him. A magic eye would follow the drawing and a pantograph in the shop would burn the required shape automatically ten times larger than on the drawing. Apart from significant savings in labour costs, the steel parts were cut more accurately. If cut by hand, it was often necessary to use a file to finish them off.

Apart from money problems, morale in the workforce had suffered, productivity was far too low and working conditions were appalling. Proper management was totally lacking. The shipyard management thought they could carry on as they had done when building the Titanic and its two sister ships. One manager I talked to said the reason for the firm's troubles was that they had given up riveting steel plates together and it had been replaced with welding. He had totally overlooked the fact that welding was much quicker to do, was stronger and also required less steel. When I talked to some of the managers I always got the same answer: 'We have always done it this way.' There was never any suggestion of bringing in new equipment or modern methods of management.

One of our consultants was helping to install a computer at the shipyard. The one chosen was an ICT 1900, which had to be input by means of punched cards. It produced so much heat that the building had to be air-conditioned.

On occasions, no work was being carried out in the preparation shop. I asked why and was told that the people responsible had not delivered any steel plates. I went outside to the plate store. The people involved were in a shed doing nothing. They said they could not work due to inclement weather. I pointed out that the rain had stopped about an hour ago. After that they started to do some work. So where, I wondered, was management?

Another time I walked through the tool room. One fitter had portraits of the Queen and the Duke of Edinburgh above his lathe, together with Union flags.

I mentioned to someone that the operative was clearly very loyal. "Not at all," said one man. "We are sure he is a Catholic and we want him out of here." A week later he had gone. They had got their way.

One manager told me he had arrived for work in the morning to find sunshine streaming in through the window. For the past 18 months the ship under construction on the slip outside had blocked out the natural light. He went outside to find that the ship had gone. It had launched itself overnight. The Navy had found it in the Irish Sea and towed it back to Belfast, fortunately undamaged.

The last liner they had built was the Canberra, later to find fame in the Falklands War. Its construction had lost the company millions. I did an environmental survey on it many years later. I was intrigued by its method of propulsion: it had diesel engines driving the electric generators which fed power to electric motors that drove the ship.

Near the end of my time at the shipyard I was asked to assist in setting up a network analysis (critical path analysis) exercise to demonstrate to senior managers how it works and its benefits. Network analysis dates from the mid-1940s and is a tool for assisting management in the planning and control of non-repetitive projects.

Briefly, it is a way of controlling activities and the order in which they should be used. If the project is drifting off course, it will tell you what extra resources are needed to bring it back on course in terms of money or manpower. It will also give you the order in which the activities should be undertaken.

I had always found network analysis to be an interesting and valuable technique. It incorporates the logical dependency of one operation on another. It uses this information to define a period of time within which each operation must be carried out, and to indicate levels of priority for management purposes. After giving my initial talk and an explanation about the technique, I had all the managers having a go at drawing a very simple flow chart.

The advantages of network analysis are that it enforces strict planning of the project, forcing realistic completion dates and cost considerations to be forecast. This technique can be used to great effect in building and construction work, launching new products, custom-built products (ships and machine tools for example), company reorganisation (such as office moves), plus repair and maintenance projects.

Using this technique, the sequence of events can be determined and crucial activities identified. As an example, when constructing a house you cannot start on the roof until the walls have been built. The roof activities would have to wait and therefore would have a long float. A float is defined as the freedom to carry out individual activities without affecting the final project. A VLCC, or bulk carrier, would have about 10,000 activities in its construction.

In shipbuilding, the traditional way was to leave the installation of the engine till late in the construction. This meant leaving part of the deck open so that the engine could be dropped in. However, network analysis showed that time and money could be saved by laying down part of the stern end of the ship's keel and then installing the engine and the engine room bulkhead. This allowed service lines to be installed to the engine as other work continued.

I left Belfast very happy to have been working in the shipyard and, fortunately, a year or two before the Northern Ireland Troubles began. It saddens me that this once world-

RMS Canberra

famous shipyard no longer builds ships and has not done so for some time. I understand it has done some repair work. The company had not realised that survival lay in a total revamp at a time of increasing competition, especially from newcomers in the Far East. At one time it had been the largest shipbuilding firm in the world.

Harland and Wolff were not the only once-thriving shipyard that found themselves in trouble. Along the Clyde, Scottish shipyards were suffering in the same way. Clyde shipbuilders had become famous for building such ships as the Queen Mary, Queen Elizabeth, Caronia, the Royal Yacht Britannia and Queen Elizabeth 2. But after World War Two, the shipping industry went into decline.

In 1968, the Upper Clyde Shipbuilders (UCB) was formed from an amalgamation of five major firms. This merger was a result of the Shipbuilding Industry Act of 1967, sponsored by Minister of Technology, Wedgwood Benn, who would later turn his attention to 'rationalising' the motor industry and initiating its decline.

Of the five firms in the new consortium, only one, Yarrow Shipbuilders, was profitable. It was hoped that the merger would turn around the fortunes of the other four. But it didn't work. Amid much controversy, the Upper Clyde Shipbuilders went into liquidation three years after its formation.

However, Yarrows had left the ship before it sank. They were only owned 51 per cent by UCB and they were not happy being part of it. So in 1970 they withdrew from the consortium. Its secret of success was that it kept its plant and equipment up to date, something that other yards had not done, or had not been able to do.

In 1999 Yarrows, along with Fairfields, became part of BAE Systems and is now the largest shipbuilder in a greatly reduced number on the Clyde. In the Yarrow tradition it concentrates on warships, although it has built cargo ships as well. Unlike many of its shipbuilding contemporaries, it has survived.

8

AFRICA REVISITED

Audrey, a great friend of mine from my days in Rhodesia, was a senior nurse. She decided to leave the country some time after me and settled in London. She also bought a plot of land in Somerset West outside Cape Town in South Africa, and built a house there as a holiday home. Her plan was to spend about a month there each year to miss some of the UK's winter and to enjoy the summer in the southern hemisphere. On many occasions I would go out with her for a very pleasant stay in a lovely and warm part of the country.

On one occasion I was staying with her at the same time as a number of other British and South African friends. We wanted to go somewhere none of us had been before and we decided on the Kalahari Desert. It covers about 35,000 square miles and its most southerly boundary is the meeting point of South Africa, Botswana and Namibia. It was not the best time to go, as there had been heavy rains in Mozambique and the resultant floods had also affected the Kalahari.

We drove in three cars from the Cape up the west side of South Africa, and met up with a couple from Johannesburg at Uppington. The road further north was a dirt road, so we parked our three cars and hired a four-wheel drive people mover for the final leg of the journey. When we arrived at the main camp, we set up our tents and unpacked our food, drink, chairs and hurricane lamps. Fortunately the camp had excellent washing and toilet facilities.

As expected, the desert was no longer a desert. The recent rains had had an amazing effect on vegetation, with grass and wild melons, which had been dormant for some time, visible everywhere.

I spent much time studying the meerkats. They looked just like the ones you see in TV adverts. Meerkats live underground in clans of 20 or 30. Fights break out between rival tribes, often leaving many dead. They also have many natural enemies including eagles, jackals, snakes and lions. The snakes are particularly dangerous. They can make their way into burrows and kill the younger ones. When they are out of the burrow, elder males stand tall, guarding and to alert of any danger. We also saw Bushmen and their wives, who were very short in height and could go without food and water for long periods of time.

Our visit proved to be very interesting for everyone. On the way back we stopped at a farm owned by the Afrikaner husband and wife who were in our party. They lived in the Northern Cape on a 10,000-acre farm. It was very poor land, supported only by some 3,000 sheep. Their house had been built by Hans's grandfather and was typical of its type, single storey with a verandah and a tin roof all the way round.

I was driving there with my friend Audrey. It was a sunny day without a cloud in the sky. Suddenly a single black cloud was heading in our direction. I realised it was a swarm of locusts. It took about five minutes for it to pass. I had to stop as the windscreen wipers could not cope. They could not throw off the bodies fast enough. When we started driving again the temperature gauge shot up. I opened the bonnet hoping we had not run out of water. That was not the cause. The front side of the radiator was coated with dead locusts. It took about 20 minutes with a stick to remove them all.

You hear of whole crops being stripped in minutes and I now understand how this can happen. When we reached the farm, Hans had seen the locusts coming and had brought out his spray and killed hundreds of them. There were about two to three inches of dead locusts underfoot.

The next morning Hans said, "Engelsmann, would you like to see a small part of the farm?" I said I would. It was very hot at the time. "How long do you think you could last out here without any water?" I asked, supposing it would be about an hour.

Hans said it wouldn't be a problem for him. "I could live off the land," he said. Hans showed me a small plant with a large corm. When you bit into it, much sweet water flowed out of it. Another plant, a bit like soya, was very rich in protein. In all, there were about four plants that would keep someone alive. This is how the Selous Scouts (crack troops) in Rhodesia lived when out on manoeuvres. They had to live off the land.

We built the braai, or barbecue, with stones covered with chicken wire. Then kindling was placed over the fire and lit, then more chicken wire. Now the meat could be cooked. There were also candle plants. Hans cut these into nine-inch lengths and placed them in a circle round us. They were very resinous and burnt with a smoky flame for about one hour.

After a pleasant stay we set off on our return journey. We headed south and spent the night at Clan William. In that area they grow grapes, not for making wine, but for producing raisins and sultanas. We arrived back in Somerset West exhausted but happy, having had an excellent and informative few days.

Then, a few years later in the late 70s, I stayed with Audrey again and this time we took a trip that was rather more dangerous. Audrey had five other people staying, some of whom had not been to the country before. Although I knew the area well, I did not mind seeing interesting places again. We planned a long trip as far as the north of Natal to Hluhwe-Umfolozi game reserves. This would mean at least a three-day drive up the N2 motorway. We planned the journey carefully, arranging three places to stay, and set off in two cars.

We were a little worried about driving through the Transkei, a former African designated homeland, but agreed that we would only drive in daylight and without stopping for a meal. Fortunately it all went well.

Our next stop was a night's stay in a rather rundown hotel at the foot of the Drackensburg mountains. Next day, we continued driving north. We entered Natal and came to a part of the road that was being re-surfaced. This meant that one side of the road was closed and both ends on the one way system were controlled by stop and go men. We just arrived before the direction of travel changed.

We travelled for some time, the only vehicles on the north-bound carriageway. We approached a bridge over the road and suddenly two masked men carrying AK-47 guns approached our cars from behind the uprights of the bridge. They stepped out into the middle of the road, preventing us from continuing our journey, and pointed their guns at us. Both were wearing face masks.

It transpired that they had hijacked a security van, blowing off the back doors, and were taking the contents to their flatbed VW Golf. The poor African driver had been clubbed and was sitting at the side of the road covered in blood, while someone attended to him. Both our cars rather stupidly did the fastest U-turns in history, almost colliding with each other.

My first thought was that the luggage in the boot would stop bullets without doing much damage, as long as it did not hit the petrol tank. Fortunately they did not fire and we had got away with it. By this time the traffic from the south was moving again. There were some big, articulated vehicles and I thought that if we got between two for protection, we could continue our journey northbound. However, this was not necessary, as the bandits, still wearing their masks, drove past us with their loot. This was the second time I have had a gun pointed at me, the first was in Yemen described elsewhere.

I stopped a car approaching from the south and asked the driver if he had a mobile phone. He tried to contact the

Safely in the game reserve

police for about 30 minutes, but there was no reply. This was perfectly normal in that country.

It was only after about 30 minutes that fear hit us. When we arrived at the game reserve, we spoke to some off-duty police in the bar. They said they were not surprised, as that sort of thing happened every week. If the men had not been wearing masks we would not be alive. Nor would we have been saved by the luggage in the boot, had they shot at the car.

Back in Cape Town afterwards, I was offered an AK-47 gun with as much ammunition as I wanted for the equivalent of £5 sterling. The Russians had flooded Mozambique with weapons during the civil war. It was then, when I saw the size of an AK-47 bullet, I realised how lucky we'd been. The bullet would have gone through the back of a car, through us and the luggage and then through the engine. None of us would have survived.

Nigeria

In 1976 I was once again reminded that different rules apply in Africa. I was asked to carry out the feasibility of a project to set up a chair-making plant in Ilorin, the capital of Kwara state in north-west Nigeria. Having obtained first-hand experience in chair making, I was looked upon as an ideal candidate for this assignment. I had not been to Nigeria before, but had heard mixed reports of life in that country.

When my plane from London approached Lagos Airport
it was told to circle for a while as there had been an attempted
coup overnight. Apparently a Colonel Dimka had led an
army uprising to overthrow the Government.

Colonel Buka Suka Dimka was commissioned as a second
lieutenant from the Australian Army Officer Cadet School in
Portsea, along with a number of other officer-cadets. In 1966
they staged an unsuccessful coup against the administration
of General Aguiyi Ironsi because they felt the country
had suffered under his administration. Then, in February
1976 Colonel Dimka led a group of army officers in the
assassination of General Mohammed for maladministration.
But their coup failed and Colonel Dimka, along with 38
other army officers, were arrested and publicly executed by
firing squad in May of that year.

The execution was shown in its entirety on television.
The commentary described, "Our brave marksman taking
aim," and then, as the men fell to the ground, we heard,
"These traitors meet their end." The film was then shown
again, forwards, in reverse and in slow motion.

I learned on arrival at Lagos that the coup had caused
our delay in landing.

The drive to the hotel had been an experience in itself.
Nigeria had recently changed over from driving on the left
and was now on the right. It became apparent that some
drivers had not realised there had been a change. Many
crashes were encountered. It was said that some drivers

had gone out the weekend before the changeover to have a practice on the other side of the road, which had caused even more accidents.

Miraculously, I arrived in one piece. I had booked into the best-looking hotel in Ilorin. The brochures had depicted a low, two-storey building around three sides of a swimming pool surrounded by attractive flowerbeds and a garden area. To my surprise, I arrived at the hotel to see that the swimming pool did not contain any water, but instead was filled with empty Whitbread's Pale Ale beer cans. These not only filled the pool area but had spilled over into the flowerbeds, killing all traces of plant life.

In my room, the taps over the basin did not give out any water, hot or cold, which seemed rather ominous. I soon found the reason why. The British, as the colonial power, had left the country with a good source of water from reservoirs and dams. When the local dam level started getting low, it seemed that no one with any authority had started water rationing. Just before my arrival the reservoir had run dry. The lack of water had only been noticed when no water came out of the taps.

Instead, delivery by water carts became necessary. Each room received two litres of water per day for everyday use, but it was not fit to drink. I soon got into a routine. The first task was to brush one's teeth, followed by a dry clean of the body. All used water was collected in a bucket and was used at the end of the day to flush the toilet. The food in the hotel was edible, but the only drink available were cans of Whitbread's Pale Ale. While I had nothing against it, I did not want to drink it every day for breakfast, lunch and dinner.

I had been provided with a Volvo estate car and driver. The first thing I noticed was that all windows and movable parts had the car's number etched on them. Apparently, if someone had a car window broken, they would steal one from someone else's car as a replacement. It took a long time to obtain spare parts from motor dealers.

When driving on many days after the attempted coup, we were stopped at army checkpoints to be searched and told to get out of the car and place our hands on the car roof. I had been reading Frederick Forsyth's book The Dogs of War, which was about a coup in a West African country. In it, he suggests that in such a situation you should look at the ammunition pouches of the soldier's tunics to see if they had been ironed flat, i.e. empty. These were flat.

The government was spreading a rumour that the British were behind the coup. We were advised to stay indoors. A few days later the rumour changed: it was not the British but the Americans who were behind it. We could then go out again.

The next few days were spent seeing what furniture firms existed in Kwara and the sort of furniture they produced. Also, I obtained information on supply sources for timber, skilled labour, covering materials and so on. The factories

I visited were small and producing chairs similar in design to some of those being produced in the UK. However the quality was very poor and clearly would not find a market in Europe. I could not find any information on exports to other African countries.

As part of my study I had to visit Ibadan, the largest city in West Africa. On my first visit I was put up in a house of one of the staff of the British Council. My stay was prolonged by an attack of food poisoning. I was surprised that this had not occurred sooner owing to the lack of good sanitation and proper hygiene.

There was a prevailing anti-British feeling and I was told that on occasions like this the mob usually broke the windows of the British Council Library. My host reassured me that the local glazier had the dimensions of the windows so they could be quickly replaced!

Once I had recovered from my food poisoning, I realised that I would have to visit Ibadan again. So I went to the President Hotel to make a booking for the following week. The hotel had seen better days and was in a rundown state, but there was nowhere else that looked remotely bearable.

There was a white woman on reception with whom I made the booking. It was apparent that some of the local staff were terrified of her. On arrival the following week I went to check into the hotel but the white woman had gone home. The local man I spoke to said that they had not received my letter and hence I did not have a booking. At that point I should have produced some money, a bribe.

I told him that I had come in person some days before and had made the booking with the woman. I asked him if he was suggesting that she was lying? He looked terrified. I told him to get her on the telephone. He hesitated, so I said he better have another look at his bookings. He said the only room they had left was a double. I said I would take it at the price of a single, to which he readily agreed. The room itself had seen better days. There were six light bulbs but only two were working, leaving the room in permanent gloom and the bedlinen was not clean.

After a few more uncomfortable weeks in Ilorin I went into Lagos to book my return trip to UK. I went to the British Caledonian Airways office and the man on the front desk told me that all flights were full. At this stage I had not told him my destination or the date I wanted to fly. I saw there was a white officer in the back of the shop. I called him over, gave him my travel plan and I was immediately booked in.

At immigration on my day of departure I was asked if I had any Naira (their currency) on me. I knew you were not allowed to take any Naira out of the country. I said I did not have any. He asked to see my wallet. He went through it and took out a £20 sterling note. I asked him why he had taken it. He said, "For me to give you your passport back." If you want to leave the country, you do not argue. Fortunately, this was the only bribe I had to pay during my stay in Nigeria.

I hope the country has mended its ways in the 50 years since my visit. It is potentially a very rich country, but clearly wealth had not filtered down to the poorer people. Everywhere you went people expected to be tipped. It was with pleasure and relief that I left that unpleasant, corrupt and insanitary country. I vowed that I would never again visit Nigeria.

9

THE PEOPLE'S DEMOCRATIC REPUBLIC OF YEMEN

I n 1974 I was told that my next management consultancy assignment would be a difficult one and I could refuse if I had strong feelings about it. The job was in the so-called People's Democratic Republic of Yemen (PDRY), based in Aden. It would be a three-person assignment in the soft drinks industry and was being financed by United Nations Industrial Development Fund (UNIDO) based in Vienna.

The assignment called for three consultants, a marketer, a production engineer and a water quality specialist. I was the water expert. Before undertaking the assignment, we had to be interviewed by an official at the UK Foreign Office. The person we saw said they did not like British subjects going to Yemen.

It was, we were told, one of the most uncompromising communist states, having been taken over by the Russians. Our UN Laissez Passé (diplomatic travel document) should give us some protection but we should not rely on it. The

UN document was, however, useful for getting an upgrade to first-class on Middle East Airlines to Aden via Beirut and on the return journey to London. Preferably we all should be single. In fact, I was the only one. We were reminded that we would be working for UNIDO and hence we were UN personnel. We should not consider ourselves British for the purpose of the assignment. Everywhere we went we would have a political shadow, known as our 'interpreter'. We should always be careful whom we talked to. We should not take a camera, and be aware of prostitutes who would try to compromise us. Above all, we must on no account try to enter the ex-Royal Navy dockyard in Aden, or the ex-RAF Khormaksar airfield. We were also told that the hotel rooms were bugged, so we should hold discussions outside, in the square near the Crescent Hotel.

Brief History

Aden had been occupied by the Royal Marines in 1839 to counter attacks by pirates on British shipping en route to India. The opening of the Suez Canal in 1869 meant Aden became an important coaling station for ships on their way to India. As British influence was further extended eastwards and westwards, Aden eventually became a Crown Colony in 1937.

In 1963 Aden and most of the other protectorate states were joined to form the Federation of South Arabia.

Independence from Britain was planned for 1968. However, in 1963 two nationalist groups, the National Liberation Front (NLF) and the Front for the Liberation of South Yemen (FLOSY) began an armed struggle against British control. The planned independence was brought forward by one year.

The Marxist NLF became the dominant party, changing the name of the country to the People's Democratic Republic of Yemen. It nationalised all industry without compensation, with the exception of the BP oil refinery at Little Aden and Cable and Wireless. There was nothing democratic about the PDRY. In fact, it became a Russian satellite.

One of the industries nationalised was soft drinks. It consisted of Coca Cola, Pepsi Cola, Canada Dry and Green Spot (Schweppes). None had been paid for the nationalisation of their plants. Only Coca Cola and Canada Dry plants were still operating.

After a while the two plants needed spares and had applied to their former owners to supply them. Both said that if they were paid in full for the loss of their plants, together with money upfront for the cost of the required spares, they would supply them. This was rejected by the PDRY government, who then contacted UNIDO to provide a team of experts to rationalise the industry and to keep the two plants going. This was our, rather unenviable, assignment.

In 1967, towards the end of British rule over Aden and

South Yemen, the Royal Northumberland Fusiliers were being replaced by soldiers from the Argyll and Sutherland Highlanders under Lt-Colonel Colin Mitchell. In June of that year, the local armed police, trained and armed by British troops, mutinied and took control of the Crater District. This area was where the Coca Cola plant was located.

As a result of the mutiny, 22 British troops were murdered. The military commanders in Aden refused to let Colonel Mitchell retake Crater to recover the bodies of the murdered men. They feared that such a move would result in further killings. Mitchell was astounded and furious. In July 1967 he led his men back into Crater and retook it with only a few shots being fired. He rescued the bodies of the murdered men. There were no further British casualties.

Mitchell was hailed as a hero by the British press. He was, however, severely reprimanded by senior officers and threatened with dismissal from the Army. He resigned in 1968 having been passed over for promotion.

The Assignment

We were given an interpreter called Abdullah, who was assigned to accompany us everywhere we went. He told us that he had been trained in Hungary, where he had learned his excellent English. Abdullah showed us photos of London where, he told us, working people lived in absolute squalor and had little to eat. In contrast, said Abdullah, people in the Soviet Union had plenty to eat and were well housed. As a Londoner, I could not recognise any of the places in the photos he had shown us. Needless to say, he had never been to London and did not want to go there. He was, however, useful in arranging meetings with government ministers and officials.

In Colonial days the soft drinks industry in Aden had been big due to the presence of British military personnel, their families and civil servants. Also cruise liners called in there to refuel and pick up supplies. We started by examining all four plants. The two still operating, Coca Cola and Canada Dry, could only be described as filthy and producing unsatisfactory and unsafe products. In Europe, health and safety inspectors would have closed them on the spot.

Fizzy drinks are produced by cooling water to 10 degrees centigrade and then pumping carbon dioxide into it. Carbon dioxide is more soluble in colder water than in warmer water. However, in both plants the cooling units were scarcely working at all. As a result, there was very little fizz when bottles were opened. Syrups obtained from the USA were no longer available to them and had been replaced by an inferior Akras syrup from Hungary.

The finished product was sold in returnable glass bottles. Before being filled, they were put through a bottle washer. I took a side panel off one of the bottle washers. Inside was a mass of cockroaches, living and feeding in the hot, sticky atmosphere. I asked the manager about the cleaning routines of the bottle washers themselves. His only answer was that they were carried out as required.

I told him that they were absolutely filthy and should be cleaned at once. His response was to place someone at the end of the line and a light bulb behind passing bottles to show up any floating cockroaches. However this proved ineffective, especially when the person supposedly checking for cockroaches was talking to his mates instead. It was quite common to find a cockroach floating in one's drink.

The water used in the product came from boreholes. Both plants had water treatment units. However, neither had worked for some time. An analysis of the borehole water showed it to be brackish and not up to World Health Organisation (WHO) standards. The sulphate content, in particular, was too high, but the only effect this would have on a consumer was the same as taking a dose of salts.

The 'white' sugar used in the drinks was supplied by Russia. I looked at it under a magnifying lens. Apart from dirt, I could see rodent hairs and droppings, and the colour was 'off-white'. I sent a sample back to the UK for a microbiological assessment. The report said it was bug-infested (i.e. bacteria), and it confirmed the presence of rodent hairs and droppings and general dirt. The report on the sugar also contained the statement 'do not eat this'. The Russians were charging £600 per metric ton of sugar, the market price for top-quality white sugar at the time, which this was most certainly not.

The staff were good at improvising. Some of the machinery parts that could no longer be obtained from abroad were made out of bits of metal and old motor tyres. Many of the workers slept on the factory flat roof. Washing facilities were rudimentary to non-existent.

A key problem for the plants was that their market had collapsed. In the past, when the British were in control, there was a ready market from British servicemen and their families, and also from civil servants. Now that they were gone, their only market was the impoverished local population.

When the Suez Canal opened again, cruise liners called in to Port Suez where they could take on board soft drinks produced to international standards in cans. These cans were infinitely better than a hardly drinkable product, in poorly-washed returnable glass bottles, from Aden.

The local people were really suffering, with beggars everywhere. More than once I heard in the markets from stallholders that 'the British must come back to free us'. I had to tell them that this was extremely unlikely.

I also heard in the markets the strains of 'Lilliburlero', the signature tune of the BBC World Service. I asked one stallholder why they listened to it. "Because they tell us the truth," he said. Among the many countries I have visited, I do not think I have ever been to a more unhappy place.

The Hotel

On arrival in Aden we were taken to the 26 September Hotel (formerly the Aden Rock), named after the day of the revolution. It had been built in the 1960s but was in a very rundown state. The rooms were adequate but needed decorating and the air-conditioning units did not work. There was, however, a new-looking radio in each room. Apart from a power line and an aerial, there was a third wire that did not seem to do anything. Being curious, I pulled this third wire out of the radio, but it continued to work perfectly. By evening it had been wired back into the radio. This was the means of bugging the rooms that the Foreign Office had warned us about.

We went to the restaurant on the top floor, which had good views of the town and the naval dockyard. For each meal we were shown to a table by an Indian waiter. However, before we sat down the waiter would wave a napkin under the table and a large rat, which had been eating the crumbs, shot up the curtains and into the air-conditioning system leading to the kitchen. Sometimes there was more than one rat. This performance went on before each meal. I asked to inspect the kitchens but was prevented from seeing them.

From my vantage point in the restaurant, I could at least see the naval dockyard from afar. It had many Russian warships at anchor, some of which were cruisers with tarpaulins over their weaponry. My uncle and godfather had been in the Royal Navy in the late 1930s and I had heard many stories about his time in Aden. I was sorry, therefore, that we had been warned on no account to enter the dockyard.

Food was very limited and largely dependent on the arrival of the latest Russian cargo ship. Hence there was little choice for a diner. The sugar in the hotel was the same contaminated product used to make soft drinks. The only place we found to enjoy a reasonable meal was the Missions to Seamen at Steamer Point. We all enjoyed the locally caught shellfish there, especially the delicious speciality of the house called 'Crap au Gratin'. I wish I'd kept the menu.

In the top-floor restaurant of the hotel, a large, round table was kept for Europeans. One evening, a Swedish sea captain joined the table. We learnt that his tramp ship, which took cargo between Port Suez and Karachi, had broken down when passing the naval dockyard. The captain had managed to park it inside the dockyard and was now staying in the hotel until spare parts arrived from Sweden. Every evening he would visit his ship to ensure that all was well.

After a hard drinking session in the hotel, the captain asked whether I would like to see his ship. I readily agreed and, ignoring what we had been told in London, entered the dockyard.

It had many Russian warships at anchor, some of which appeared to be cruisers with tarpaulins over their weaponry. I assumed them to be missile launchers. We walked through the main gates of the dockyard, getting a friendly wave from the Russian guards, and then boarded the captain's small boat to take us to his ship.

As we approached, I noticed a number of small boats waiting near his ship. Each one contained Russia naval officers. They knew that the captain had a good supply of schnapps on board and they were there to help him drink it.

Now I had joined the party. I do not speak Russian and they could not speak English. However, by about 2am, and having consumed a large amount of schnapps, we were able to communicate. I vaguely remember that we agreed that, if left to us, we could solve all the world's problems.

I returned to the hotel about 5.30am, not feeling too well but somehow aware that my working day started at 6.30am. I also realised that I had broken one of the Foreign Office's most important rules.

On another evening we were joined at the European table by a Scotsman who did not want to talk about his work, apart from saying that he was in the import/export business. I had come across such people in Africa and knew that someone in import/export was really making money by exploiting a war or crisis. I was not wrong.

At the time, PDRY was at war with Oman over a border dispute. The Sultan had appealed to the UK to supply them with officers for their army and pilots for their airforce. The Omanis were in the middle of upgrading their airforce with Hawker Hunter fighter planes.

A few nights later I was woken by a noise in the street outside. I went down to investigate. A number of low loaders were passing by, with the Scotsman directing the traffic. The cargoes were covered by tarpaulins, but I could see they were carrying aircraft, with the wings parked alongside the fuselages. I recognised the planes by the shape of the tail fins. I said to the Scotsman, "I now know what you mean by import/export." He had bought the planes to sell for a large profit. "One has to live, laddie," was all he would say. By morning he had gone and so had the planes.

In the evenings, the hotel restaurant was turned into a nightclub. At about 10pm, the belly dancer came on to do her act. Afterwards she liked to sit with the British. She said that when the British were in Aden she had been very friendly with many soldiers and officials. They had a special name for her, they called her Coke Up. Unfortunately she made straight for me. I remembered the Foreign Office's warning about 'tarts'. Was this one of the prostitutes who would try to compromise us?

After a while, a rather drunk young Cuban, one of a contingent training the secret police, tapped me on the shoulder and told me to leave as he wanted to sit next to the belly dancer. I did not move, so he pulled a gun from his waistband and stuck it my ribs. I did not think he would pull the trigger, but as he was drunk, I thought he might do it by mistake. I did not hang around to found out, but left rather quickly. At least he saved me from the belly dancer.

On Monday and Wednesday evenings the British Embassy held parties on their flat roof. It was known as the Embassy Club. Hungarian, Polish and Czechs attended frequently, but East Germans, Russians and Cubans did not.

Apart from a drinks party one evening, entertainment also included a film screening and some Scottish dancing. It amused me to see Eastern Europeans attempting to dance Scottish reels. The ambassador told me that, apart from providing entertainment, the parties were a good listening opportunity for the powers-that-be.

A very pleasant Czech diplomat told me that he had spent an extremely good time in London when stationed in the Czech Embassy in Kensington. He told me how the Russians listened to conversations in bugged hotel rooms, and advised me where it was safe to talk freely.

Being a Muslim country, we had Fridays off but worked the other six days of the week. We finished work at about 2pm and often went to Gold Mohur Beach by taxi for a swim and sunbathe. Fortunately the beach was protected by a shark net.

It was always a hazardous journey getting to the beach as the drivers were often 'high' from chewing qat, a drug made from a local plant. Just to add to the danger, the cars had not been maintained and the tyres were bald. However, Gold Mohur was an oasis in an otherwise rather unpleasant place.

Eventually we completed our report for the PDRY Government. It did not make comfortable reading. The factories were in a very rundown state, with equipment that needed replacing. They were also filthy, producing drinks that were unsafe to consume. The raw materials used to make the drink were either unsafe (sugar), or inferior (syrups). Since water treatment plants were no longer operating, water used in the manufacture was below WHO standards, particularly due to high sulphate levels.

As expected, our report was not well received by PDRY Government. I felt sorry for the local population who had to put up with such an appalling regime and way of life. The market for soft drinks that had previously existed had now gone. It was good to leave such an awful place.

At the end of the assignment we had to report to Canada Dry in Beirut. I had not been to Beirut before so I thought I should learn something about Lebanon's history. It had been under a French mandate since 1945, after which independence had been obtained. Since independence, periods of political stability and turmoil had alternated. During that time Beirut had become the financial and trade centre of the area.

The governance of the area was split between the Maronite Christians and Shiite Muslims. In 1948 Lebanon supported neighbouring countries in attacks on Israel. As result of the war, 100,000 Israeli Palestinians fled to Lebanon. After the war the Israelis would not let them return home.

In 1958 Lebanese Muslims started an insurrection, intent on making the country a member of the United Arab

Republic. In 1975 a full civil war broke out. A coalition of Christian groups were on one side and PLO, Druze and Muslim militias on the other. At the time of our visit in 1974 the extremes between the wealthy and the poor were evident everywhere. Our assignment completed, it was with some relief that I headed home.

10

ARABIAN GULF

I n 1978 I was approached by a representative of the Shell Oil Company and was asked if we would be interested in carrying out a survey of oil pollution in the Arabian Gulf. The Arabs thought that oil tankers, when deballasting (shedding water into the sea), could be polluting the gulf. Our client would be Abu Dhabi Petroleum Limited (ADPC). Shell was the lead company in a consortium of all major oil companies and was acting on behalf of ADPC. The Gulf Arabs are traditionally fishermen. They were worried that, when the oil had run out, they could be left with a contaminated gulf, preventing them from returning to their traditional way of life.

Jebel Dhanna was the main crude oil loading port in the United Arab Emirates (UAE). Existing deballasting regulations at Jebel Dhanna UAE marine terminal required ships' masters to certify that their ballast water was clean before discharge into the sea. It was not known, however, if the state of cleanliness of the water met the standards required under regulations of the UN agency International Maritime Consultative Organisation (IMCO, now called IMO).

Tankers could clean their tanks whilst 100 miles or more from land using a technique known as 'Load On Top'. In this process, tanks that had contained oil are washed with sea water, and the wash water transferred to a slop tank.

More recently hot seawater under pressure is used, followed by COW (crude oil washing) to remove oil residues. When tanks have been washed the oil/water in the slop tank is allowed to settle and the lower water layer released into the sea. The oil layer is then pumped to a cargo tank where it forms part of the next oil cargo.

The oil companies were under pressure to install shore reception facilities whereby ballast water would be pumped ashore for oil removal, and clean water would then be returned to the Gulf. At the time of our visit, the oil camp at Jebel Dhanna consisted of an airstrip and largely single storey buildings for accommodation, offices and recreational facilities. There was also a golf course of sorts.

A team of four went out to the UAE, consisting of myself and three qualified chemists. We hitched a lift to the tankers with some of the pilots based out there. Their job was to fly out to Das Island, about 20 miles north east of Jebel Dhanna and rendezvous with an incoming tanker. The pilots were responsible from bringing tankers from Das Island to Jebel Dhanna. Parts of the gulf are very shallow, and it needed

The Taiei Maru

an experienced pilot to supervise this journey.

Once we'd got our ride out there, transferring from the pilot boat to the tanker was not always easy, depending on the tanker's size and age. Some had a gangplank which we could walk up. Others had a rope ladder which they would lower to us and then use to haul us aboard. A choppy sea was particularly tricky for boarding. Whilst the tanker remained stationary, the pilot boat was thrown around both vertically and horizontally. You had to judge your moment and jump. We also had to transfer onboard all our equipment. We decided to work in teams of two.

Once onboard, the first thing to do was to place your palm on the earthing plate to remove any static on your body. Then we would meet the captain and explain what we needed in order to carry out our work. Our task was to take samples of ballast water during the ship's deballasting. Discharge of ballast water takes place below water level, so samples had to be taken from the cargo pumps themselves. To start, we visited the control room to ascertain which tanks were to be deballasted and the cargo pumps to be used. These pumps are situated just forward of the engine room bulkhead and above the bilges.

Then we visited the pump room to find out where samples could be obtained from the pumps to be used. On average samples were taken at half-hour intervals. Samples were collected in 1.1 litre glass bottles to which hydrochloric acid was added immediately to prevent the growth of bacteria. Samples were airfreighted back to London for analysis to determine their oil contents. The method used was that laid down in IMCO Resolution A.393 (X). Briefly, the oil monitoring system referred to applies to any approved system to verify that the oil content of the effluent does not exceed the stated level.

Over a six-week period, 44 tankers were visited and sampled. These could arrive at any time of the day or night, and so we had to be available round the clock to set out from the shore. Only five tankers were missed during this time as our teams were already sampling other ships.

Results showed that samples from 10 ships were satisfactory, i.e. all had less than 15 parts per million (ppm) of oil in all their samples. Three ships showed levels of oil above 15 ppm in all samples. The remainder showed one sample above 15 ppm during deballasting. The most polluting ships were the three smallest and oldest vessels.

Based on our results it could be shown that, at the current level of activity, the amount of oil entering the Gulf from deballasting operations during our six-week survey was below the level at which installation of on-shore reception facilities would be necessary. Our report was well received by everybody except ADPC. The most polluting ship was their own. We also had to record details of the ship and its activities about its previous voyage and its more recent activities.

As a result of the work carried out, I was made a consultant to Shell Tankers UK. I discussed this study with IMCO who also invited me to become a consultant for their organisation. To their knowledge, a similar study had not been undertaken anywhere in the world before.

After our work in UAE, my colleague Nick Billingham and I decided we would break our journey in Cairo as neither of us had been there before. When we went, in 1978, Cairo and Giza had not been developed as it is today. Now new building work comes close to the pyramids, which previously had been open country.

My first assignment for Shell was to go through one tanker from each of their classes and do a similar operation. The first of their tankers to be visited was the Limopsis,

Dr Nick Billingham

Step Pyramid

an ultra-large crude carrier (ULCC) and the third-largest tanker in the World.

I set out from Jebel Dhanna with the pilot to Das Island for the tanker's journey back to Jebel Dhanna to load one third of its cargo. The gulf is very shallow at that point and, due to its size, the tanker would have gone aground if it had taken on more oil.

We then set out for Ras Tenura in Saudi Arabia to take on more oil. However, halfway there the ship anchored in the middle of the gulf, where it remained for the whole day. I could not understand why we had stopped. The Captain then sent for me and said his orders had been changed and we were not going to Ras Tenura, but instead we were going to Kharg Island in Iran.

At that time, Iraq and Iran were at war with each other. What I did not know was that if a ship goes into a war zone the crew get double pay. I would have doubled my fee if I only had known.

The first thing to do was to black out the ship. I helped by taping black bin liners over portholes. We arrived at Kharg Island with the tanker completely blacked out as it entered the loading port to take on the cargo.

The dock had anti-aircraft guns mounted at either end. Shortly after our arrival the guns opened up. Fortunately it was only a practice, possibly a display for our benefit. However, the captain was worried that the flashes from the tracer fire could cause a fire on board. I realised that, as my job was in the pump room, about six decks down, there would be little chance of escape if the ship had been attacked.

During one of my breaks I made my way up on deck for fresh air and met the Iranian pilot. He was handing out propaganda leaflets and posters saying 'Death to the Aggressor'. I noticed that he spoke English with a slight Scottish accent. I asked him about this. He said he had been to Strathclyde University, obtaining a degree in marine engineering, and had met his Scottish wife there and brought her back to Iran.

Once we had loaded Iranian heavy crude, we started loading Iranian light. As much as possible was loaded, but as dawn was rapidly approaching, it was time to go. My job was now to help take down the bin liners I had been busy putting up some hours earlier.

Once back in the open sea the Captain apologised, saying there had been no way for me to get off once the orders had been changed. That's why I'd had to remain on board. To make up for the 'inconvenience' he had sent for a helicopter to take me back to Jebel Dhanna. In due course a helicopter landed on the deck and I got in.

A short while later I met up with the Limopsis again. This time it was in Lyme Bay in the English Channel. Shell had been concerned that taking a tanker the size of Limopsis through the English Channel could pose a risk. Tankers of that scale are simply too big to enter certain ports, necessitating a cargo transfer at sea. The idea was to transfer the cargo into two smaller tankers moored alongside. One would then go to a British port and the other to Rotterdam.

Lyme Bay and Southwold had been identified as convenient places to conduct test transfers. The authorities in Lyme Bay were worried that such an exercise posed many risks. The Dorset coastline is of major importance to the local community, principally for fishing and tourism. A major oil spill would have a devastating effect on this community and also on the wildlife, leaving oil-coated fish and birds washed up dead on the beaches.

Hence my job was to see whether the transfers on this occasion did pose a problem. I was glad to be able to report that the operation had gone ahead without any trouble being caused. I never heard whether these transfers went ahead on a regular basis after this trial.

My taxi back to base

Boat deck

Two boats alongside each other

11

PEOPLE'S REPUBLIC OF CHINA

Having been made a consultant to the International Maritime Organisation (IMO) following my assignments in the Arabian Gulf, I was asked in 1980 if I would be interested in carrying out a project for them.

China had recently joined the United Nations and at the same time oil had been discovered in the South China Sea. They were keen for IMO personnel to provide training in oil-spills prevention, containment and clean up. They had put together two teams of young marine experts, all fluent in English, for training. One team was to visit firms in Europe and the other team to visit USA and Canada.

I was selected to set up and lead the European team and an American, George, would lead the North American team. Initially, our jobs were to set up study tours to visit suitable firms and organisations in our respective areas. Once this was done we were to rendezvous with the UN office in Tokyo for final briefing.

I was met there by a Mr Tatsuki, a young man who welcomed me and asked whether I had been to Japan before. I said I had not, but I was very pleased to be in Tokyo. He then asked George whether he had been to Japan before. George replied, "Yeah, I came ashore in 1945 in a tank landing craft and knocked hell out of you bastards." George then commented to me that they didn't seem very friendly.

"I am not surprised after a remark like that," I replied.

George and I then flew to Beijing to meet the teams. Mine consisted of seven people – five men and two women. To my horror the youngest of the men was 58 and the oldest 80. The two women were in their 50s. They were certainly not the marine expert team I had been promised, being neither young nor fluent in English. The team leader of my group was Professor Wu. He could speak some English, but Mr Fang had a better command of the language. The remaining five had virtually no English at all.

George and I were staying at the Beijing Hotel, which dated from the first half of the 20th century and was in a very rundown state. Each of us was provided with an 'interpreter' and a policeman to accompany us everywhere we went. We weren't allowed to leave the hotel on our own.

The first evening we were invited to have dinner in the Beijing Duck, a government-run establishment to welcome foreigners to the country. Presiding at the dinner was the Minister of Communications whose department included environmental affairs. He gave a welcome speech through an interpreter, which took over one hour. He then sat down and his deputy said the same thing through an interpreter, this time taking 30 minutes.

Everyone present then looked at me, and I realised that it was my turn to say something. I spoke slowly so the interpreter could keep up. I said that it was very nice to visit China and to take my party of Chinese round some countries in Europe. This would help them to learn about how the West handles such problems involving oil spills, prevention, containment and clean up.

Everyone then looked at George, but before he could say anything the Minister apologised for the snowy weather, which was due to a cold wind blowing down from Siberia.

"Gee, I guess nothing good ever comes out of Russia," said George, whereupon everyone started applauding. There was a coolness between the two countries at the time. George then turned to me and said, "Did I get it right?"

"Yes, George, you did this time," I replied.

The next two days we went sightseeing, accompanied by our interpreters and policemen. We started off with a visit to the Summer Palace, then the Forbidden City, then on to the Great Wall and finally the Temple of Heavenly Peace.

In between these visits we were shown many temples, which had been done up externally but were still a mess inside. As my fellow sightseer George said, "I guess when you have seen one you have seen them all." I knew exactly how he felt.

The Forbidden City ramparts

As interesting as these visits were, I really wanted to see parts of Beijing unaccompanied. But we had been told that we were not allowed to leave the hotel on our own. One afternoon I told my interpreter that I had a headache and needed to rest. I watched him from my balcony, standing with his bicycle and looking up at my window.

After about an hour he had obviously had enough and left. I waited for a further half hour and set off. I went downstairs and waited until the concierge had left his post for a few minutes, then left. Crossing over the main road I headed down Wangfujing Street. No one gave me a second glance although I seemed to be taller than all other males.

I wanted to buy a Chairman Mao-type cap. I had been to the Friendship Store with my 'interpreter' and tried there for a cap but without success. The Friendship Store was the only place foreigners could buy Chinese goods, and they only took hard currency. I was told that caps, as worn by Chairman Mao and his followers, could not be bought by foreigners and I should buy a cap in my own country. I did, however, buy a litre bottle of Gordon's gin.

Now that I was out on my own, I wondered if I would have more luck. I entered a large department store. It was extremely bare with no carpets or floor covering anywhere. The hardware department was situated on the ground floor as you entered the building. I expected to find tools and other items for DIY in the home. However, there were tractor wings, crowbars, sledge hammers and other heavy items that the average person would not buy.

I went up to the third floor and found the menswear section. There were caps and tunics on wooden display heads and torsos. But they were khaki and I wanted slate blue. The only way I could find what I wanted was to go round to the other side of the counter and open drawers. I still have my Mao cap; it cost the equivalent of 25 pence.

I then flew with my seven new friends on a China Airways (CAAC) plane to Teheran. The plane was a Russian-built airliner, a copy of the UK VC10 with four engines in the tail. The interior was covered in dark green and maroon fabric, which made it look like an Edwardian railway carriage.

The four engines left a black trail of unburnt fuel and could only fly at about 400 mph. I was intrigued that it had a tail wheel as well as a nose wheel. Apparently, when on the ground, it could tip up if too many people were in the back of the plane.

I felt in need of a drink and asked one of the stewards for a gin and tonic. "No alcohol," he replied. Then I remembered that I had a litre of Gordon's gin in my hand luggage. I ordered an orange juice and added it to the gin. At that point a party of German businessmen nearby also tried to order alcoholic drinks, but were similarly refused. They then became very friendly to me.

They persisted and eventually the pilot sent them a half-full bottle of red wine, which presumably he had been drinking. One of the Germans said to the steward, "If he has to drive a terrible plane like this, he had better keep it." I was then asked where I had got the gin from? I relented and gave them some.

CAAC was not a member of IATA at that time so it did not have to abide by their rules. When we were about to land people were standing in the aisle and looking for their luggage in the overhead lockers.

When we had landed safely in Teheran, having had little food, we found we had missed our connection. The plane had not flown fast enough. We stayed the night in a hotel before flying on to Paris in the morning by Air France.

We arrived in Paris to find that it was a public holiday.

What worried me was that one of the Chinese was carrying a Gladstone bag that he would not let anyone else carry. I asked him what was in it and he eventually opened it up, revealing 17,000 US dollars. This was their spending money for the trip. We checked into the Holiday Inn at Charles de Gaulle Airport. Next day, after a visit to the Chinese Embassy, we toured Paris.

The following day I took them to Thomas Cook on Rue Haussmann to exchange the money for traveller's cheques. They were worried when the cashier took the money, thinking it had been confiscated. They had never heard of traveller's cheques since very few Chinese people at that time travelled abroad. I managed to convince them that the money was safe but now in a different form.

Before I left London I explained to IMO, who had financed the trip, that my schoolroom French was very rusty. I was told not to worry as the Chinese Embassy in Paris was providing an interpreter. This was true, but he was Mandarin-French, which did not help me at all.

Our first visit was to a firm in Vernon, northwest of Paris. I had spent the previous night with a dictionary trying to put together my thanks to the company in French. At the end of it, one of their employees came to me and said in perfect English that my speech was very good but he had a few suggestions to make. In fact, he had rewritten the whole thing. This proved to be very useful as I was able to use it at the end of every visit we made in France.

Our next port of call was to see IHC in La Rochelle. This firm made small craft that acted like a Hoover, scooping up oil/water emulsions known as 'chocolate mousse' and caused by spilled oil and sea water. Having scooped up the chocolate mousse, their craft treated it in order to break up the emulsion and then returned the water phase to the sea.

Further visits were made to French firms making booms to stop the spread of oil after a spill, skimmers for picking up oil from the sea and detergents to break up chocolate mousse. We also visited the Port Authority of Le Havre and Antifer, and also Serep and Kleber, which were both involved in anti-pollution measures.

We then took the hydrofoil to Southampton. Our first visit was to BP on the Isle of Wight where they were producing small units for picking up small quantities of oil (as shown in the picture below). Then back to the mainland and visits to two firms in the Southampton area, Dasic and Rotork, which were involved in the construction of specialised anti-pollution vessels and in oil spill clean up.

The group was then interviewed on Southern Television. This should have been simple enough, but we experienced a problem before the interview even started. Professor Wu said he would be the spokesman for the group, but the producer said his English was not good enough. He said that Mr Fang and myself should do the talking. The programmes went ahead but the professor was suffering from a bad case of loss of face.

BP units for picking up oil

Le Havre Trip

Whilst we were in Southampton, the team said they wanted to visit Marks and Spencer. Some of the men were very amused by the women's frilly knickers on sale. I was told they would not be allowed to buy them or there would be trouble bringing them in to China.

We then travelled to Liverpool to visit a small firm, Water Witch, making vessels for generally keeping docks and ship berthing areas clear of pollution. Before we went, I was contacted by the Chinese Embassy saying that the second secretary would like to accompany us on the trip. I told them that I would have to get permission from IMO. The answer came back that they would have no objection.

When we arrived at our hotel in Liverpool, I was unpacking in my room when the telephone rang. It was the concierge. He said there were two officers from the Special Branch of the Metropolitan Police who wanted to see me, so would I come down immediately. I could not think why they would want to see me. I went down to reception and met the policemen. I was asked if I had in my party a member of Chinese Embassy staff. I said the second secretary had accompanied us.

What I did not know was that, at the time, Chinese Embassy staff were restricted to remaining within 30 miles of London. I had broken this rule and was told that I was in real trouble. The poor individual was driven back to London in a police car.

I immediately contacted IMO to let them know what had

happened. To my amazement I heard nothing more from anyone and assumed that IMO had pulled a few strings in Whitehall. After visits to two more firms in the North West, Dunlop and Hoyle Marine, we returned to London.

I had to take our party across London by underground during rush hour. When the train arrived I told them to get on. I pushed two onto the train and dragged another one with me. When the doors closed there were four people missing. The remaining Chinese were being polite and saying 'After you' to other people wanting to board the train. Then the doors closed and they were left on the platform. At the next station I told my three to get off and stay exactly where they were on the platform. When another train arrived, there were another two of the party, whom I pulled off the train.

I then became extremely worried. There were still two Chinese adrift. Not having been to London before, they did not know where I was taking them, or the name of the hotel we were heading for. Fortunately, after another two trains came and went, I had collected all seven. With much relief I conducted them to the Grosvenor Hotel at Victoria Station.

After visiting another three firms involved in oil pollution prevention and containment, we flew to Rotterdam in the Netherlands to see the port authorities, followed by Hydrovac, also in Rotterdam. Now that we were in Holland, I said that I would show the party Amsterdam, one of the great cities of Europe. But I received a message from the

Chinese Embassy saying they did not want that. Instead, I should take them to see fields of turnips. They said it would be better for them seeing turnips rather than just buildings.

I replied that I insist that I show them around the city. In any case, I did not know whether turnips are grown in the country. Did they mean tulips? I did not receive a reply so we went ahead, starting with a rondvaart, a trip round the canals. The commentary on the boat was in four languages. When we approached the Oude Kerk, the commentary said, "This is the centre of the Red Light area."

"What is 'red light'?" asked the professor. I explained back in the hotel.

When it came to dinner time, the professor said that he had a headache and did not feel like eating. He was much better at breakfast and had a broad grin on his face like the Cheshire Cat. I think the whole group knew what their leader had been up to the previous evening.

After Amsterdam we travelled to Delden to see Servo Chemische. We then travelled to Trelleborg in Sweden for two days, followed by another couple of days in Oslo and Bergen in Norway.

I went to check in at the hotel in Bergen I had booked, only to be told that the Chinese Embassy had cancelled the booking. A member of the Embassy's staff turned up and told me that the programme had been too intense and members needed to rest. I pointed out that IMO was paying for the study tour and the visits would continue. I explained the position to the hotel manager and fortunately he managed to find us accommodation.

I spoke to them as a group and they all said they wanted to continue and could not understand why the hotel booking had been cancelled. Before our next visit I hastily arranged a boat trip round the fjords. This was much appreciated. In the evening we boarded the ferry to Newcastle.

The North Sea was rough for the trip, and nearly all members of the group fell ill and took to their cabins. However, the professor, the 80-year-old and myself decided to stay up all night. The old man was intrigued by one-armed bandits, which I suspected he had never seen before. I think he made a small profit.

The professor and I had many drinks as I wanted to talk to him about life in China. Each time I had tried to talk to him during the trip, all I got was the Chinese party line. But after many drinks he said that he hoped that before long he and Mrs Wu could once again go back to dancing the tango. Apparently this was currently banned. This was my only opportunity on the whole trip to learn about life in China. He said he looked forward to the time when they could live in a free and open society, similar to the one he had experienced in Western Europe on this trip.

We all returned to London and after a few days boarded a flight from Heathrow back to Beijing. Fortunately this time it was a Boeing 747 and not a Russian plane. When we were nearing Beijing the professor came and sat next to me, clearly in some distress. He produced a small box and asked me if I would bring it through the diplomatic channel at Beijing Airport. I picked it up and it was quite light. I told him that I could not do that.

When we arrived at Beijing Airport I said goodbye to the group and they were herded into an army lorry. At that point my political shadow/interpreter arrived to meet me. I went to pick up my briefcase and next to it was the professor's small box.

I told my minder that I must say goodbye to the group and clambered up into the army lorry. I went to the far end, putting my briefcase and the box down.

I then went round the members of the group shaking each one by hand. I then collected my brief case, leaving the box behind. To this day I do not know what was in the box. However its lightness suggested to me that it was probably frilly knickers for Mrs Wu, a memento from Marks and Spencer in Southampton.

All in all the trip went very well with only a few minor hiccups, and the party members were very appreciative. It was a great experience for them and, in most cases, their only opportunity to see the outside world. It was also a good trip for me, but it left me not really understanding them. For instance, at each place we visited, all they wanted to eat was Chinese food, they would not try anything else. At each restaurant we visited the Chinese staff greeted them in Mandarin like longlost friends. My immediate thought was that they had means of spying already in existence that could work to our detriment.

Each evening they needed at least one hour to write up their notes. I assumed the notes would contain details of what they had learned that day. I discovered later that they had to write notes on the behaviour of each fellow member of the team. On more than one occasion during visits to host firms, we seemed to lose one of the party. They were under orders to study aspects of the firms outside their brief. For example, the central heating system, details of forklift trucks and any automation. It was becoming like industrial espionage. They were abusing our hospitality and that of our hosts. I told them if this continued I would send the person involved back to China. Luckily this hadn't been necessary.

China

12

ENJOY YOUR STAY

t was 5.20pm on Maundy Thursday, the day before Good Friday, in 1984. Nearly all the staff had left our environmental consultancy to start their Easter break. There was only myself and Len, one of my co-directors, left in the building.

The telephone rang and, since there was no one left in the office, I took the call. It was the general manager of one of London's five-star hotels. He said that the hotel had received a message from an anonymous caller saying that LSD (lysergic acid diethylamide) had been put in all the hotel's water tanks. LSD is an illegal drug that produces hallucinations.

The manager said he had called the Metropolitan Police but they could not help as they had more important things to deal with. As an interim measure, the hotel had provided each guest room with bottled water and a note telling guests not to drink the tap water.

The manager's next step was to look in the Yellow Pages

for firms that could possibly help. He tried many, but no one one was prepared to help. Our consultancy, Voelcker Science, being at the bottom of the list, was his last chance of finding someone who could help. By this time the manager was desperate. If he had been unable to find anyone, nothing could have been done until the day after Easter Monday. I said we would help and told Len he could not go home.

The manager explained that there were 16 water tanks in the roof space. I asked him to let us have a two-litre water sample from each tank and also the tanks' dimensions. Tank sizes were necessary, so that we could calculate their volumes, and I asked for the details to be telephoned to us. Water samples should be biked over to us as soon as possible.

In the meantime, I looked up details of LSD in the Merck Index. This is the chemist's reference book, which gives details for all the major chemicals, their formulae, source, physical properties, uses and toxicity. I was interested in finding the solubility in water of LSD and hence the lowest dose that would have any effect on people drinking the water. I discovered that LSD is not very soluble in water. With this information and knowing the volumes of water involved, I was able to calculate the least amount of LSD necessary to achieve the perpetrator's warped objective.

The next step was to find the current street value of LSD. The Daily Telegraph Information Section is a mine of information and it was to them that I directed my enquiry. I had to convince them first why I required this information. They soon called me back with a price.

Armed with the street price for LSD, the volumes of water involved and the solubility of LSD, I was able to calculate that it would cost a minimum £50,000 to have any effect. The chances of this being a hoax seemed strong, as no ransom had been demanded.

An hour and a half later, the 16 water samples arrived and Len and I set about carrying out the analyses. It took about one hour to complete the work. We found nothing unusual in any of them. We had also included four other popular recreational drugs of that time, which also were absent.

I was then able to telephone a much-relieved general manager and inform him that all samples were uncontaminated and therefore safe to drink. We were able to submit a substantial invoice for the work, proving the point that if you are prepared to help a client in trouble with prompt service, the fee charged is of secondary importance to them.

In working out the bill, I took into consideration that the work was carried out in after-hours overtime, also on a Bank Holiday long weekend and finally that it was urgent and that public health could have been involved. The manager said he thought our invoice was very reasonable. When a client says this, it usually means that you could have charged much more.

Expensive Guests

We had a call from another five-star hotel in London. A number of guests had complained about a chemical smell in their rooms and in the passages. The smell was quite strong and was recognisable as a fluid used in dry cleaning. I visited the area where dry cleaning and laundry were carried out and the same smell, but stronger, was immediately recognisable. It was obvious that the ventilation system was not working properly. It was therefore a job for a ventilation expert to improve the system without polluting the air outside.

On entering the building I noticed that there were a number of Gulf Arabs in the foyer. I asked the under manager, who had showed me round the dry-cleaning area, how much they charged to stay in the hotel. He told me it would be £120 per night. However, for Gulf Arabs like the ones in the foyer, the charge was £1,000 per night. They were restricted to the first floor. I asked him how he could justify discriminating like that.

He said, "Come and have a look." He took me up to the first floor and showed me one of the rooms. The arms had been broken off a sofa, mirrors had been smashed and in the bathroom a plumber was removing a smashed basin and lavatory bowl.

He told me that the carpet was a write-off and a certain amount of redecorating was also necessary. The room I saw was not the only one in such a state. He told me about a young Arab prince who had recently booked in for 12 weeks. He had paid £84,000 in cash in advance. They knew him of old as he had stayed before. He rarely went out but invited in a number of prostitutes for his entertainment. He also ordered vast amounts of alcohol.

There were so many rooms left in an appalling state that the hotel had had to set up a joiner's shop to repair furniture. They also had to employ full-time electricians, plumbers and painters to carry out the remedial work. After these costs were taken into account, there was not much profit in it.

Standing Room Only

A few years ago I was invited by a friend to attend the Royal Scottish Corporation's annual dinner, held at Grosvenor House in Park Lane. It was held appropriately on 30 November, Saint Andrew's Day. Gentlemen were required to be dressed in kilts or black ties as appropriate.

My friend had known the host for a long time. He was called Hamish and owned a large mansion in Scotland set in a few thousand acres. Hamish had been blind from birth but that did not stop him from leading an active life. He also liked showing visitors round his large house and explaining who were depicted in the family portraits.

Unfortunately, the portraits had been rehung in the wrong order following spring cleaning. So Hamish's commentary no longer fitted in with the actual picture being viewed. A great aunt he described now appeared to have a splendid beard.

At the start of the evening the Moderator of the Church of Scotland said grace. We could then sit down. The problem was, our table for 12 had only 11 chairs. I was the unfortunate person left standing without anything to sit on. After a while someone at the next table, referring to me, said, "Do you think he is going to make a speech?"

There was a member of staff in a green jacket strutting about, so I went to him and said I didn't have a chair. He said, "Can't help, all staff are busy serving the first course." There did not appear to be any member of staff who would listen to my plight. I even went into the kitchens seeking help, but no one was interested, or could speak English.

I looked around and noted a grand piano with a stool on a raised platform.

Later that evening, Kenneth MacKellar was going to sing with a pianist accompanying him. Could I possibly take the stool? I decided this was not really an option.

However, I then saw Lord Forte, whose company owned the hotel at that time, was sitting at the top table. I saw the green jacketed man and asked him again for help. "I am too busy taking wine orders," he replied. Fortunately I was bigger than him. I grabbed him by his jacket lapel and pulled him in the direction of Lord Forte.

"I am going to ask your boss for his help since you have

been completely useless," I threatened.

"If you do, I could lose my job," he replied.

"You certainly deserve to, you have been absolutely useless." I pulled his lapel even harder, which did the trick. A chair was produced in a matter of seconds.

By this time I had missed the first course but was in time for the second.

Hamish was sitting next to me and insisted on serving himself with vegetables. A few potatoes and peas landed in my lap. I was in no mood to enjoy the evening. By this time I felt angry and just wanted to go home.

We then had Andy Stewart performing some lighter music such as 'Donald, Where's Your Troosers', and encouraging everyone to join in.

Whereupon Hamish got up and did a Highland Fling. I must say he did it very well. However, there was suddenly a gasp from some of the women present.

He had answered the question, 'What does a Scotsman wear under the kilt?' In Hamish's case, the answer was nothing.

Star Wars

During my management consulting time I spent nearly two years working in the South African branch of the company. In early 1970 my mother came out to visit me and see something of southern Africa. I was living in Bryanston, a white suburb predominantly populated by English-speaking people. It was some way out of the city centre and fairly empty during the working week. I therefore decided to book my mother into a five-star hotel in a suburb for the first four days, which was much closer to the centre. This suburb also had a large shopping centre close by, with a full range of shops.

My mother had not flown before or been anywhere recently outside Europe, so it was a real adventure for her. She was travelling on her own because my father refused to fly. He said that if the good Lord had intended us to fly he would have given us wings.

Fortunately she had a medical doctor sitting next to her on the plane. At one stage she wanted to go to the toilet. She let herself in but did not lock the door properly. She was busy making a paper seat cover when someone burst in. All her hard work was in vain. The paper seat flew into the air and she had to start all over again. Fortunately the newcomer showed how to lock the door properly. For someone in her sixties who had not flown before and was travelling on her own, she did very well. We were then joined by my brother John who was spending some time in southern Africa on his way home to the UK from Australia.

For the first four days of my mother's stay I had to work. On the third day I received a telephone call in the office from the South African Police. They asked me to come urgently to the hotel as there had been an incident. I arrived wondering what on earth could have happened. I found my mother sitting on the bed looking distraught, with Sergeant Hofmeyer conducting proceedings.

He said to me, "I can do nothing with this lady." I asked him what the problem was and he replied, "She will not tell me her age."

"It has nothing to do with you," declared my mother.

"Without it I cannot proceed," said the sergeant. "So I ask again, what is your age?"

"She's 64," I said.

"Thank you, we can now proceed."

The under manager explained that there had been a burglary overnight. Both my mother's rondavel and the next one had been broken into and goods taken.

A rondavel is a round building with a thatched roof, based on an African mud hut, but luxurious, with onsite facilities and air conditioning. I noticed that, although the window was fitted with burglar bars, the adjacent entry door had been hung the wrong way round, i.e. the hinges should have been on the other side away from the window. It was therefore easy to open the Yale lock by putting a hand through the burglar bars, undoing the lock and letting yourself in. The next door rondavel had the same fault.

My mother had lost all her jewellery. She had brought too much with her, as we had, on my father's side, some well-heeled relatives, who she was going to see during her trip. A cousin of my father's had been sent out to South Africa from Britain to set up Imperial Chemicals South Africa in the 1920s. He was a well-known character and friends with many of the top names, from Harry Oppenheimer downwards.

The next-door rondavel was occupied by a Lloyds underwriter, who had lost everything. On the day of the burglary, he had packed all his possessions because he had been told he was to move to another rondavel the next morning. The thieves had gone off with his luggage, leaving him with nothing to wear, so he had to borrow the under manager's suit.

At the time, another consultant in my firm was carrying out an assignment for the Hotel Board in Pretoria, the nation's capital. Many star systems for grading hotels of any size existed around the country, and the Board wanted a common system to apply nationwide. Even a hotel with only one star would have to have adequate security. This was to work in our favour.

I telephoned the hotel manager telling him that my brother and I wanted to see him. We went along next day and were confronted with one of the most unpleasant men I had ever come across. He had come out from the UK after the war, having been commissioned in the RAF, and he thought he could lord it over everyone. Although his was a wartime commission, he had kept his RAF rank of squadron leader, which only regular officers were entitled to do.

On entering his office there was an African man on his

knees polishing the floor. The manager kicked him hard up the backside and said, "You, out." Before I had a chance to say anything he said, "If your mother is stupid enough not to have taken out insurance don't come in here looking for money. She is not getting a rand out of me."

"You had better listen to what I have to say," I replied. "I notice the hotel has a five-star rating. You are on the point of losing all of your stars. You are currently trading illegally and could be prosecuted. I am surprised that you can be running a hotel that is not safe for anyone to stay in."

When he asked what I meant, I said, "On the basis of my mother's rondavel and the one next door, anyone could get robbed or attacked."

I told him about my fellow consultant working for the Hotel Board in Pretoria and how his job was to design a single star system to apply nationwide. On that basis, I explained, his hotel would be unable to operate since it would shortly lose all of its stars. "Even a small hotel or guest house has to have adequate security, something you do not have."

At that point the manager got up and left the room. Presumably he was going to check what we had been talking about. I began to wonder if he knew how unsafe some of the rondavels were. When he returned he said, "How much do you want?"

Before our meeting, my mother and I had worked out the value of the jewellery she had lost. At the time there were two rands to the pound. I became rather confused and came away with too much money, but I was not sorry. The police had said they expected to make an early arrest. However, I heard nothing more from them.

We were going to Durban and on our way we stopped in Pietermaritzburg, the capital town of Natal, and found the best jeweller. My mother, who had been shaken by the whole experience, was starting to regain her composure and threw herself into buying replacement jewellery. I saw recently on the internet that there were no longer any rondavels at the hotel where my mother had stayed.

13

WHERE THERE'S SMOKE...

Tobacco kills more than eight million people every year and its use is one of the world's biggest public health issues. According to the World Health Organisation, nearly 80 per cent of smokers live in low to middle income countries.

Tobacco has its origins in North and South America and was widely used by the native peoples. The Northern American Indians thought smoking a cure for syphilis, as did the Spanish sailors who returned home infected with the disease.

Sir Walter Raleigh acquired the habit of smoking tobacco from natives in North America and was probably the first person to bring the idea back to Britain. He considered it a cure for indigestion and aches and pains. During the Great Plague of 1665, people in London came to believe that smoking tobacco was a way of preventing the Black Death. At Eton and other boarding schools, smoking every morning was encouraged. In fact, not smoking was a beatable offence. By 1880 cigarette smoking was widespread and had been taken up by women. Smoking had become a fashion statement.

Tobacco and its products are now recognised as being the leading causes of preventable diseases. It can affect the brain, increasing blood pressure, causing respiratory diseases and affecting heart rate. This is largely due to absorption of nicotine, an alkaloid that affects the central nervous system. Cigarette smoking is responsible for about one third of all cancers, mainly lung cancer, and is also a cause of emphysema and bronchitis.

Before the 20th century, lung cancer was extremely rare. It was not until 1929 that a link was suggested between cigarette smoking and lung cancer, as well as other diseases. It wasn't until 1960 that a definite link was established.

This did not stop the cigarette companies from continuing to make health claims in their advertisements. Footballer Stanley Matthews allowed his name to be used for advertising Craven A cigarettes which, according to an unknown actress in a 1952 advertisement, "Does not affect your throat." It was also claimed that Craven A cigarettes were "made especially to prevent sore throats." Meanwhile, a Kensitas advert aimed at overweight people told them to avoid meals and, instead, smoke a cigarette.

In 1962, when I emigrated to Southern Rhodesia, I took a job with British American Tobacco (BAT) as a costing clerk. Then BAT was ordered by their head office to set up a quality control laboratory. So after two months with the company, my role changed from costing clerk to be back as a chemist. I had not declared my university qualifications when I joined the company, but my secret had leaked out. For me it was easy to set up a laboratory, buy equipment, recruit staff and train them to operate it. We were told to use the methods laid down by Head Office in London as standard. Four months later, when the laboratory was running well, I decided to seek a better job. I never thought my rather brief experience in cigarette making would be useful later on.

Back in the UK in 1971, I had decided to branch out with a chemist friend as environmental and food safety consultants. One of our clients was an international firm of loss adjusters. I was asked to assist with a claim in Kobe, Japan to provide a scientific input following the January 1995 earthquake.

The claim involved a warehouse storing cigarettes. The building had been badly shaken but remained intact. However, racks containing large outer cartons of individual 200 packs had largely collapsed and these, together with loose cigarettes, were scattered over the floor.

The warehouse was temperature and humidity controlled. However, the power supply had failed as a result of the earthquake and the insured was claiming that, apart from the physical damage, the cigarettes were unsaleable since controlled conditions had not been maintained.

I took samples of unopened boxes of 200 cigarettes and also loose cigarettes from the floor, placing them in plastic bags for testing in the UK.

I then went shopping in Osaka for the same brands as the ones stored in the warehouse. I was fortunate in finding a shopkeeper who could speak English. He told me that the principal brands in the affected warehouse had been withdrawn from sale a year or two earlier. Hence those in the cold store were old stock. I therefore bought samples of the two top brands currently on sale for comparison purposes.

Back in the UK we conducted smoking tests (smoking by machines under controlled conditions and collecting the smoke for analysis) and also tested for tar, moisture and ash content. The results showed there was little difference between the two groups, the subject of the claim and those currently on sale.

My report was submitted to the loss adjuster and forwarded on to their insured. I had a great feeling of achievement when I heard that the insured had withdrawn their claim.

Our firm occasionally provided scientific advice for the Insight Team of The Sunday Times on some of their investigative work. They were preparing an inquiry into the activities of British American Tobacco. The resulting article, which appeared in the 19 May 1990 edition, includes this quote: 'BAT said it did not agree that cigarette smoking was addictive. Thousands of people in this country give up smoking every year.'

The Sunday Times asked us to carry out tests springing from another quote in the same article: 'BAT claims the tar content of two brands sold in Kenya, Embassy Mild and State Express 555, are comparable to those sold in Britain.' Having carried out the tests, we found that the tar yield of Kenya's Embassy Mild was over double that of its UK counterpart. Ten Cent, one of BAT's cheaper Kenyan brands, had a tar content greater than the 23mg of Britain's Capstan Full Strength. The average British tar content is 13mg. The results of our tests showed that Embassy Mild cigarettes in Kenya were much stronger than those on sale in the UK. The article appeared as a double page spread. It gave the name of our practice and also my name.

The following Tuesday I received a telephone call from one of the directors of BAT. He said they took a poor view of my input in the article. He said that their tests had not shown any link between cigarette smoking and cancer.

I said in that case they should employ skilled researchers not incompetent ones. To deny the link between smoking and cancer, established over 30 years earlier, was criminal. I asked him, "Have you ever thought how many people you and your firm have been responsible for killing?"

He then said he wanted to meet me to discuss our test results. I pointed out that he should be talking to The Sunday Times since they had commissioned the work, written the article and had paid for the tests carried out.

I said that if he wanted us to repeat the tests we would do so at their expense. He then asked me what test methods we had used. I told him that, as a qualified chemist and an ex-employee of BAT, I had been responsible for setting up and commissioning the BAT laboratory at their factory in Rhodesia.

The methods we had used in this investigation had been their official ones, which I had used when I worked for BAT. That put an end to the discussion.

He simply said, "Oh," and rang off. I thought, Game, set and match to me.

A short time later, Readers Digest commissioned me to do an article about tobacco, cigarette smoking and its effect on human health. I was happy to oblige.

Kobe cigarette warehouse subject to earthquake damage

14

TRAVELS DOWN UNDER

When I was semi-retired I wanted to go travelling, particularly to countries that have warm climates. I had been to Australia on business, but had only really seen parts of Sydney. So in 2003 I decided to see more. I booked myself on a package holiday and was able to visit many of Australia's main tourist destinations.

Then I went back three months later to have a closer look at places of interest with a view to emigrating. The idea was to keep a place in the UK, too, so that I could avoid winter altogether by spending summer in a different hemisphere. I particularly liked Adelaide, the capital of South Australia and also Brisbane, capital of Queensland. Adelaide was described to me as being full of old people and churches. I did not feel I was ready to join them just yet. Brisbane, on the other hand, had a real buzz about it. It was the fastest-growing part of the country and had overtaken Perth as the third-largest city after Sydney and Melbourne. For me, it had to be Brisbane.

On my return to London, I obtained emigration details from Australia House on Strand. Being over 55, I could apply for a retirement visa as long as I met certain requirements.

You must not have a criminal record, which meant obtaining a certificate to that effect from the Metropolitan Police. Jokes about convicts and Australia did not go down well.

You must have a minimum of £70,000 in assets and be in receipt of an income of a minimum of £17,000 year.

You must in good health. My blood pressure was on the high side, but a visit to my GP and a prescription to control blood pressure solved this problem. The Australian doctor whom I saw in London asked me if I had any tattoos. I said I did not. He told me to take off all my clothes so he could have a good look. "You are right," he said.

"If I'd had any, would it have made any difference?" I asked.

"It would not have enhanced your case."

The other condition for acceptance was that you must agree to join a private medical insurance scheme so that you would not be a burden on the state for any medical problems.

It was then a question of waiting, in my case for about nine months. By then, I had obtained details of a new property development on the Brisbane River. I put down a deposit, not realising that, at the time, there were rules governing foreigners buying property in Queensland.

Firstly, at least half of the purchasers of any development must be Australian. Foreigners could only buy brand-new properties, or off-plan. This was to help give locals a chance to buy, so that they were not excluded by an influx of foreigners. A foreign buyer also had to get permission from the Foreign Investment Review Board (FIRB) in Canberra before purchase. Then, when you come to sell, you could only sell to an Australian because the development was no longer brand new.

By 2004 I had satisfied all those requirements and I bought a two-bedroom, two-bathroom unit, with an open-plan living area. Being on the ground floor, it had a large deck outside which was big enough to hold a party for up to 60 people.

As a newcomer, I found it easy to fit in as the locals were very friendly. The development had an excellent swimming pool with a lounge overlooking it. Any flat owner could hire the lounge for a party, company meeting, or for any event requiring furnished space with cooking facilities.

Once I had established myself in my unit I thought I should become an Australian citizen and hold dual nationality. I went to see a migration consultant and told him what I wanted to do. He listened to my story and then said, "Not a chance mate, you are too bloody old." I asked whether there were any exceptions. "Two," he replied. "The first is having children who have migrated before you." I hadn't.

"What's the other?" I asked.

"You could always marry a Sheila." I told him I would bear that in mind.

I was keen to explore islands of the South Pacific, and Brisbane was an ideal starting point. I visited New Zealand, Fiji and Vanuatu many times, and also Western Samoa and the Cook Islands less often.

I particularly liked New Zealand. I was always intrigued by the way many of them pronounce their E as an I. On the ferry from Wellington to Picton in the South Island, a voice would announce over the tannoy, "Would all travellers with cars make their way to dick seven and get into their vehicles ready for arrival."

A geyser in Roturua, New Zealand

It was a vowel sound that could cause much amusement. I was staying with some Kiwis I had met in London who were very hospitable and lived in Picton. On one evening I was taken by my hosts to a place called Blenheim in Marlborough County not far from Picton. I met a guy called Roger there. He told me he had just built his dream house. "I have four bedrooms, three bathrooms and a really big dick. I would love you to see it."

"Roger." I said, "I don't think we want to hear about or see your big dick."

"It's lovely," he said, "it goes all round the house. I hope I can show it to you."

"Roger," I said, "this is getting worse and worse." I started laughing and Roger was looking puzzled.

"I don't know why you are laughing," he said. "I can sit out there on my dickchair."

The penny finally dropped. "Oh, deck," I said.

"That's what I said – dick."

It was in New Zealand's South Island when I had my moment of madness. It was February 2002 and I was 66 years old. I was on a tour that stopped in Queenstown for a few days. On the first day we came across Kawarau Bridge, a bungee-jump site. I had always been intrigued by bungee jumping and wondered what it would be like. I had a good look. I thought about it a lot.

In the morning I asked the hall porter to book me a bungee jump.

The Author in full flight

"For you?" he asked. "Aren't you a bit old for that?"

"Just get on with it," I said.

Myself and about 20 other people travelled in a mini-bus to the jump site. There was total silence on the journey as we all contemplated what was ahead. Once there we all had to be weighed and our weight written on one hand. This allowed them to adjust the rope accordingly. We could choose whether we wanted to stay above the water, touch it, or get dunked. I opted to touch the water.

I walked out on to the bridge with a young German called Oliver, who was in his mid 20s. I thought that Oliver was looking rather scared so I suggested he went first. One of the operators asked where the rest of our group were. I told them that one had changed his mind and decided not to do it. All the others had made a mad dash to the toilets.

Then it came to my turn. The operator counted to five and said, "Go." If you didn't jump first time, you were given two more chances. If you still did not jump you had lost your money. I knew that if I did not go on the first count I would not do it. So it was first time for me. It was all over in about 20 seconds, having bounced about four times. When I had stopped bouncing I was lowered into a captive boat and taken to the shore. I was so exhilarated that I walked up to the office and said I wanted to do it again. I was told that I would have to pay again, which I refused. They said I could go again for free if I did it naked. I decided that this would not be a good idea. There

After trying to throw a boomerang with little success, our teacher gave me a left-handed boomerang and I made some progress

were many Japanese watching and taking photos but not taking part. One spectator said to me, "You realise your photo will be all round Japan by now."

I particularly liked Auckland in the North Island. It is the financial centre and, like Wellington, is a beautiful city. I have always been interested in Auckland's harbour bridge and its history. It had used to have two lanes in each direction and the city council were looking at ways to increase its carrying capacity. A number of schemes were suggested: build another bridge alongside it, or demolish it and build a bigger bridge. However, a Japanese engineering firm said it would be possible to widen the existing bridge and their scheme was adopted. The piers were widened at road level and an extra lane was provided at both sides. The bridge is now known as 'The Nippon-Clip On'.

The West Coast

When I decided, finally, to sell up and leave Australia, I thought that I should take the opportunity to see as many new places as I could before I left. I had been to Perth and Fremantle, its port, a few times, but I had not travelled up the west coast further north. So I booked myself on a bus trip up the coast as far as Monkey Mia, just short of Carnarvon.

After a four-day drive we arrived at our destination, where our accommodation was in well-equipped, comfortable rooms. Monkey Mia is a popular marine reserve famous for the bottle-nosed dolphins that swim nearby. I asked one of the locals why it was called Monkey Mia, knowing there were no monkeys in Australia. The chap said, "Well mate, when the first settlers arrived, they took one look at the locals and said, 'Strewth mate, there are bloody monkeys here.'" The truth is that no one is sure exactly how the name originated, but some think that the Mia part comes from the Aboriginal term for home, and that Monkey derives from a ship or the pet monkeys owned by the Malay pearlers who lived and worked in the area.

Every morning the wild dolphins came in to be fed, which was quite a spectacle. But the thing I remember most was the swarms of flies everywhere. I bought a strong anti-fly aerosol and a hat with corks hanging from it. I thought these hats were a joke, but a slight nod of the head kept the files on the move. The only trouble was that when you took your hat off, you continued to nod your head.

I was amazed how self-contained the resort was. They could receive all major TV channels and their electrical requirements were supplied by wind turbines, while fresh water was obtained from boreholes.

We then made our way south, stopping at three pretty unforgettable places, though I do remember having excellent shellfish to eat on the way. Our first stop was to see an extraordinary display of ant heaps. These natural mounds are produced by termites and, as the picture shows, they can build up to over 10 feet tall.

The largest place we visited was a town called Geraldton. It has a memorial to HMAS Sydney, a ship sunk in World War Two. The Sydney encountered a German Q-ship (an armed raider) and they both sank each other. There were no survivors from the Sydney but a few from the German raider. In recent years the wrecks of both ships have been found on the sea bed. It appeared that the German ship was sunk by a huge explosion. It is not known whether this was as a result of the damage it had suffered, or whether it was self-inflicted, possibly on Hitler's orders.

Monkey Mia

Monkey Mia

Then we made our way back to Perth, which is a lovely city but very far away from the rest of Australia, being nearer to Jakarta than Sydney. After Perth I made my way to Adelaide on the Indian Pacific train, a disappointing journey that I describe elsewhere.

15

CROCS, YACHTS AND BOOMERANGS

As part of my plan to see as much of Australia as possible, I went north from Brisbane through the Sunshine Coast up as far as Cairns and Port Douglas. I joined a party of people travelling up the river from Cairns to a crocodile farm. Although numbers of crocodiles in the country were increasing, they were protected and it was illegal to kill them. If, however, they had been attacking people or were a nuisance, they could be shot. The crocodiles were of the saltwater variety. These are much bigger than freshwater ones and more fierce, probably rivalling the Nile crocodiles.

When we arrived at the crocodile farm, we were first taken to a large, circular, tranquil-looking pond. "Anyone like a swim?" enquired our guide. There were no takers. He then stamped firmly on the bank of the pond with his foot and at least 50 snouts and eyes surfaced and looked at us. Apparently they are sensitive to noise and vibration.

A croc

The picture shows one that approached us.

Our guide told us that these animals were either crocs that had been causing trouble in the rivers, or those born in captivity and kept for breeding purposes. When a female is ready to lay her eggs, the keepers watch the land where she lays them and mark the spot where she buries them. When mum is away from the nest, keepers dig up most of the eggs, leaving just a few buried.

This is a very dangerous activity and it takes two to carry it out. One stands by with a gun in case an extremely violent crocodile returns before they have completed their work. The removed eggs are put in an incubator to hatch.

We were shown two pens containing crocodiles that had been hatched in incubators and then kept at the farm for about three years. They are bought by Gucci and other fashion houses, mainly for making handbags and belts.

We were also shown a pen that was being cleaned by a keeper using his hose to also keep away a very large crocodile. As the keeper was perhaps aware, crocodiles can survive for a whole year on only two meals, but prefer to eat more regularly.

On another occasion, I went out in a large catamaran from Cairns and sailed down the coast to Townsville, which takes about three days. There were about 60 people on board and to start with we travelled along the Great Barrier Reef. We had a marine biologist on board, who gave some extremely interesting talks.

On the first day, one of the crew asked whether anyone would be interested in doing some scuba diving. About 30 people, including me, said they would like to do it, but 29 of us were total novices. "No experience required," reassured Jim, "just follow me." We were then asked to sign a piece of paper, effectively exonerating him if anything went wrong. After that, many people decided they did not want to do it after all. Jim was left with only four people, including me and the girl who had done it before.

"Any questions?" asked Jim. I had noticed that he had a nasty scar on one of his thighs. I asked him how he had received that. "I fell off my motorbike."

Whereupon other members of the crew started laughing, so I assumed it was not true. I thought I could see teeth marks round the wound.

"Are there any sharks?" I asked.

"A few," he replied. "No worries mate, I will look after them. There is only one problem, if you are dressed in black and look like a seal you could be in trouble."

"Well," I said, "I have just put on a black wetsuit as you suggested."

"No worries mate, they only attack in the early morning or evening. It's 11am now so we should be alright."

At that point, the other guy in our four decided it was not for him after all and got out of the water rather quickly. One of the girls did the same, leaving just me and the girl who had done scuba diving before. I told myself I could not chicken out now.

It was not very deep at our dive site, about 25 feet, so the sunlight could penetrate to that depth, giving glorious colours to the reef.

Jim said, "Don't touch anything unless I touch it first."

We set off and it was like a wonderland. The colours of the coral, the fish and other creatures were amazing. We came across what looked like grey-green grass with luminous tops. Jim poked it with a stick and it was as if someone had thrown a switch.

Then, just as quickly, the luminous tops went out. Next, we came across a large clam about two feet wide. Jim poked it and it immediately closed up. I thought it would be easy for an arm or leg to get caught in it.

It was an amazing experience and I was very glad I had not missed it. However, I must say I did keep looking over my shoulder to see if I was being followed by a shark. After about 20 minutes we had to come up because our air supply was getting low. Although the dive was enjoyable, I was pleased to return to the boat. On the way back to Townsville we stopped for the night off Dunk Island, which is very beautiful.

Another memorable excursion was going out in a large catamaran from Port Douglas to a fixed platform moored permanently offshore. The boat then became part of the structure for the next few hours. On the way out to the platform, the man in charge of the catamaran told us the reef was named Agincourt, "Where the Poms fought the French."

"And won," I added.

"But I do not know when that was," he said.

"1415," I ventured.

He turned to me and said, "Why are you such a f***ing know-all?"

"Because I have been to school," I replied.

If you travelled a short distance further out, you came off the continental shelf where the bottom is many fathoms deep. It felt safer to be above the water rather than in it. There were many stingers (Portuguese Men of War) in the

Agincourt Reef fixed platform

water. You could hire a wetsuit, but people were still being stung around the neck and hands, which can leave you with a nasty wound. I decided to see the area in a submarine and a helicopter, the latter proving to be far more interesting.

Another time I flew to Hamilton Island in the Whit Sundays, the southern end of the Great Barrier Reef, to learn to sail a yacht. I had previously sailed in dinghies and windsurfers but nothing larger. To my surprise, a yacht was much nicer and easier to sail. In a dinghy, if you 'pinch', or get too close to the wind, you stop dead and the sails flap. Whereas a yacht has about a ton of lead as the keel, so it gives sufficient momentum to pick up the wind again.

We also had an echo sounder for the depth of water under the keel, and binnacle and compass for direction. We sailed round many islands in the Great Barrier Reef, which I found fascinating. I must say that on these trips the mosquitoes were very troublesome, especially at night.

Our training yacht

The author

16

GREAT TRAIN JOURNEYS

I have always been interested in train journeys, and steam locomotives in particular. My interest stemmed from an experience in 1939, three weeks after the start of the war, when I was four years old.

The whole family, apart from my father, left London to stay with an old schoolfriend of my mother's. Me and my two brothers, along with our nanny and my mother, travelled up from Euston Station to Carlisle on the last train to have a restaurant car during the war. I remember clearly that the train had a job getting up Shap Fell in Cumbria and they had to call for a banker, another locomotive, to give it a push.

We were staying in a lovely house about 10 miles south of Carlisle. The train line, Carlisle to Settle, passed at the bottom of the garden, and I spent many hours watching the trains go by.

His interest has remained with me all my life and I am now a shareholder in the Bluebell Line in Sussex, and the Great

Central Line from Loughborough to Leicester, which is the only privately owned dual-track line in the UK. I am also a part-owner of seven restored full-sized steam locomotives. I have learned to drive two of them under supervision, one is a 2 6 4 tank engine and the other is a 4 6 2 Pacific named 257 Squadron, a Battle of Britain class locomotive. These are shown in the accompanying photos.

The Ghan

In 2011, I decided to take a look at Darwin, the only Australian capital city I had not visited. When I told my Australian friends they said, "You don't want to go there Rob, it's a terrible place." One went so far as to say, "The Japanese bombed it in World War Two, a pity they didn't do a better job." They were referring to the 60 or so air attacks suffered by the city. But there was more devastation to come in 1974 when Darwin was almost completely destroyed by Cyclone Tracy. The damage was so severe that 30,000 of its 43,000 population were rehoused in other towns and cities around Australia.

The male population of Darwin didn't inspire rave reviews either. When I arrived, I was told there were many more men than women living there. The saying among the women was, 'The odds are good, but the goods are odd.'

Having ticked off Darwin on my Places To See list, I was looking forward to the next part of my journey on the Ghan. This famous train runs from Darwin in the Northern Territory due south to Adelaide, capital of South Australia. The name is a shortened form of Afghanistan and it originated from the camels imported from Afghanistan to carry goods and people across the Continent. Camels can exist for a long time without water, and they are the only beasts of burden that were able to carry out this work.

The original Ghan ran on a narrow-gauge track of 3ft 6in and went as far as Alice Springs. This was replaced by a standard-gauge track of 4ft 8.5in but it still went no further than Alice Springs. It wasn't until 2001 that work began on an extension further north to Darwin. Previously, Australia

The Ghan at Alice Springs

had traded almost entirely with European countries and this was served by the port of Fremantle on Perth's west coast. Then, as trading shifted to the Far East, it was hoped that a train link could help Darwin serve as a trade link with Asia, as well as encouraging visitors to the area. The extension from Alice Springs to Darwin was completed in 2004.

The railhead at Darwin is about 10 miles south of the docks. Hence, once unloaded, goods have to be shipped by road to the railhead and then loaded on to trains. When I arrived there to start my journey, the railhead lorry park was almost empty and I was told that Fremantle was still the preferred port.

The Ghan at Alice Springs

I was looking forward to my three-day trip on the world's longest passenger train. The celebrated 1,850-mile journey through Australia's red centre promised some spectacular sights and with several bars and restaurants on board, it was a most comfortable journey. On my last evening aboard, I was put at a table with three Americans. One woman was extremely large and the other one was very slim, so they fitted well together in the seats opposite. Next to me was a man aged about 40.

It was the time of the American primaries, which determine presidential candidates for the forthcoming elections. The man turned to me and said, "Aren't you fascinated by our primary elections?"

I replied that, from the point of view of a UK citizen, I found them incredibly boring.

"They are all part of the democratic process," he said.

"I look forward to a time when the USA truly becomes democratic," I replied. "If it is necessary to have a war chest of at least $100 million, you have to be rich or have many backers, such as the motor industry, armaments industry, the Jewish community, or you would not get anywhere. Hence the ordinary person would not have a chance of running for president."

"OK, OK," he said. "How much do you need to run for prime minister in your country?"

"You have to put down £500 to be a candidate for Parliament. If you get five percent or more of the vote you get your money back."

I was then asked which American president, in my opinion, was the best. I said that without a doubt it was President Truman. He was self-made and came to power on the death of President Roosevelt – without a war chest. He got the United Nations into the Korean War by wrong-footing the Russians. A motion was put to the Security Council that the other members knew the Russians would veto. They did and then walked out. With the Russians absent, the UN then voted to support South Korea, which was being invaded from North Korea.

Amid such spirited political debate, we made our way to Adelaide. The first part of the old Ghan has been retained as a private heritage railway that runs 12 miles north of the city. Operating on a narrow-gauge track, it is steam hauled and has old wooden carriages. It was very interesting to see what travelling used to be like before the new standard-track was built.

Indian Pacific

After my journey up the West Coast of Australia, I stayed a few days in Perth and then took the Indian Pacific train to Adelaide. Operated by the same company as the Ghan, its sister train has similar locomotives and carriages. It had not been operating for a while because of flooding along the route. I was a Golden Kangaroo, i.e. first class.

Indian Pacific

Before dinner on the first evening I went to the bar and ordered a gin and tonic. "No gin," said the rather unpleasant steward.

"In that case I would like a vodka and tonic."

"No vodka," came the curt reply.

I suggested that the Red Kangaroos (second class) might have some gin or vodka. Apparently they didn't. I asked what he did have. "You can have a beer."

When dinner came I asked for a glass of Sauvignon Blanc, preferably New Zealand. That got him going. "What's wrong with our Sauvignon Blanc?" he demanded. In the end, I settled for the Aussie wine.

"What's your account number?" asked the steward.

I said I did not have one.

"You can't have a drink without an account number."
After an argument I eventually got my drink. He obviously
did not like me, nor a party of Canadians who were getting
the same treatment. His rudeness went on at every meal.

For the first lunch I ordered salmon. It had obviously
been reheated a few times as it was hard, curling up at the
edges and no longer pink.

"You complaining again?" he asked. It was impossible to
talk to him without being ignored or getting a rude reply.

Our journey continued, across the Malabar desert, which
was very uninteresting and much the same for miles on end.
On our penultimate day, I was waiting in my cabin for the
tannoy to announce that lunch was being served. At 1.30pm,
having heard nothing, I went along to the restaurant car to
find everyone eating.

"You are late," he said.

"Your tannoy is not working in my carriage, so get it
fixed," I replied.

On the last day he came round smiling and handing
out a questionnaire to everyone. He said he would be back
shortly to collect them. When he did, he asked me if I had
completed the questionnaire. I said that I had.

"Could I have it please?" he asked.

"No," I replied. "I have given an account of this appalling
trip and your rudeness, which was a complete disgrace. I am
posting mine when we reach Adelaide." I knew that if I had
handed it to him it would not have reached the company's

office. I could see he realised what this meant, but there was nothing he could do.

It was a pity, as it should have been a good trip. It was amazing that one man could create such a bad atmosphere, ruining the trip for me and others. This train was as bad as the Ghan had been enjoyable and it was hard to believe they were both operated by the same company.

When I was in Queensland, I took a train trip that was memorable for all the right reasons. From Cairns I wanted to travel up the coast further north. My destination was Kuranda, a rainforest village that's home to many aboriginals. To get there, you can either travel over the forest by cable car or take the train.

I chose the scenic rail journey. The train runs on narrow-gauge track and dates from the 19th century. In those days trains were pulled by steam locomotives and it was first used to transport minerals down to sea level. Now it's diesel-hauled and is a major tourist attraction. The scenery is spectacular and it is well worth a visit.

Another interesting steam railway in Australia is Puffing Billy, east of Melbourne in Victoria. It travels through the Dandenong mountains and rainforests. The railway is over 100 years old. Trains are steam-hauled and run on a narrow-gauge line. It was built to serve two areas to the east of Melbourne, where it was presumed new suburbs would be built. This never happened. However, the railway has proved to be an excellent tourist attraction.

Kuranda Station

Kuranda Station

17

EXPLOSIVE SITUATIONS

Methane is an odourless gas and the lowest member of the alkane series, which also includes ethane, propane, and butane. Methane is formed when carbon-containing materials are broken down in anaerobic conditions, in other words, when air is not present.

This happens, for example, in landfill sites. When organic materials such as paper, wood, food waste and so on are buried, the first step is aerobic digestion (in the presence of air). This means that aerobic bacteria attacks the organic materials, producing carbon dioxide and water vapour.

However, when all the air is used up, anaerobic digestion starts to take place, producing carbon dioxide and methane. Although methane is odourless, the gases produced often have an unpleasant smell due to the reduction of sulphur-containing materials also present in the waste.

Modern landfill sites are designed to collect the methane and use it. I know of sites that have an electric generating plant running on the methane produced. Methane is also present in some disused coal mines.

Apart from being a useful source of fuel, methane has an unfortunate property of being very explosive. To cause an explosion you need a source of methane between five and 15 per cent in air and a source of ignition. A spark is enough.

I was asked to visit the site of an explosion in a building on the English south coast. The site was a bowling club that the local council had allowed to be built on a disused landfill site.

There is nothing wrong in building on such sites as long as precautions are taken during construction. These consist of piling through the unstable ground, which shrinks as the refuse decays, to natural ground. Then comes the construction of an impermeable concrete slab, containing a plastic membrane at its centre, to sit on top of the piles (load-bearing foundations). All services in and out must be brought in above the slab so that no holes are made through it.

On examination of the bowling club, it was clear that none of these precautions had been taken. Holes had been cut through the slab to allow services to pass through it. Services were therefore brought in through the slab and the holes around the pipes sealed with mastic. Unfortunately, mastic shrinks as it dries, which left gaps between pipes and the concrete slab.

The main bowling hall was large and airy and had much through traffic in the form of people moving around.

Lavatories and the kitchen, on the other hand, were dead ends, with no through traffic and many pipes passing through the slab. One lady bowler, having finished her bowling went to the ladies toilet, hung up her woods, sat down and pulled out her cigarettes.

She struck a match to light up and this was followed by a large explosion which brought down the internal walls. Fortunately she was not badly hurt, but shocked and a little singed. She was screaming with embarrassment at being in full view of everyone. Though too late to spare her blushes, the problem was easily solved.

When things go wrong

Problem Solving

I was asked to find the source of a methane explosion in a new development near Liverpool Street Station in London. The building had underground parking and below that a gym. A member, having completed his workout, lit up a cigarette in the neighbouring changing room. A small explosion had occurred, but fortunately no one was hurt and little damage done.

The gym and changing room had a concrete floor, rendered walls and no sign of any combustible material, such as wood. I contacted the gas supplier, who said they did not have any gas pipes at that depth. I then went through the method of construction with the people who had been involved. The concrete floor was constructed from a very useful material, consisting of a honeycomb of cardboard contained between two layers of hardboard. It is very strong, often used for casting concrete slabs in-situ and in difficult areas. But over a period of time it gets wet and disintegrates to a slurry. I reported to the clients that this material seemed to be the only source of organic material and must therefore be the culprit. They were sceptical and said, 'Prove it.'

I set about trying to prove my theory. I obtained two different densities of the material and placed them in anaerobic jars in triplicate, making six jars in all. An anaerobic jar consists of a robust plastic shell, closed with an

An anaerobic jar showing pressure build-up

air-tight lid, fitted with a pressure gauge and a sampling tap (see photograph).

At the time we were working on several landfill sites which were actively producing methane. We took a sample of ground water to provide the anaerobic bacteria. About 10ml was added to each of the six jars, together with sufficient boiled-out distilled water to cover the samples of organic material. Finally, each jar was purged with nitrogen to remove all air and the tops were then fitted.

We waited anxiously, with daily inspections, but nothing happened during the first two months. The builders were getting worried that I was wrong in my conclusion.

Then, during the third month, one of the jars showed a slight increase in pressure, as indicated by the pressure gauge, followed by all the other five a week later. I opened the tap of the first jar and applied a match. A flame shot up about a metre in the air. The presence of methane in each jar was confirmed by gas chromatography, which separates chemical components to determine the exact amounts present. We were very pleased that we had proved conclusively how the methane in the gym and changing room had been produced. Fortunately, the client's faith in us had been restored.

We worked on many sites in the London Docklands once their use for berthing and unloading ships had come to an end. Some of the old docks were being backfilled to increase the land for redevelopment. But after a while it was realised that, in doing this, the resulting land gain had reduced the value of the site. People like to look over water and so buildings with this advantage can command a much higher price.

It was decided that one of the backfilled docks should have the top two metres of fill removed and a shallow lake created. The dock in question had been partly filled with fly tipping after it had been drained. Tests showed that methane and carbon dioxide were being generated from the tipped rubbish due to anaerobic conditions existing.

To make it safer, the top of the remaining rubbish could have been capped with clay, which would then act as a barrier and contain the methane. However, this would have allowed methane to travel laterally, possibly ending up under new buildings, which may not have been built with anti-methane precautions installed, as in the bowling club mentioned earlier.

We wanted to recommend a barrier that would collect any methane and dispose of it safely. We suggested that the top of the remaining rubbish, at two metres below the surface, should be compacted and lined with a plastic honeycomb material, usually used to provide vertical draining channels to remove surface water. This would be laid horizontally across the top of the fill material. The upper face of this material should be sealed using either impermeable plastic or clay. The ends of the honeycomb material would lead gases away from housing, for safe disposal in the air.

Building on landfill sites can be done and is being done, but strict precautions, like those mentioned in the bowling club story, must be taken to prevent methane ingression into buildings.

Fire and Smoke

Over the years we were called upon by loss adjusters to provide the scientific input into claims for damage caused by fire and smoke to products and raw materials. Our role in these projects was to advise the loss adjuster and not to talk to the insured directly, unless asked to do so.

Thorpe's Dictionary of Applied Chemistry defines smoke as, 'A dispersion of any form of finely divided solid or liquid particles in a gas, usually taken to mean the suspended matter emitted due to combustion'. British Standard 1747 describes smoke as 'finer material which tends to remain suspended in air, but can be collected by filtration. Such material is commonly known as smoke, and in extreme cases can limit visibility or cause blackening of buildings or clothing'. Larger particles, called soot, which are not suspended in air, fall rapidly due to their larger mass.

Clearly if a product has been damaged directly by fire or water there is no argument that the goods are unsaleable. Many of our projects, however, involved smoke damage. Depending on the goods involved in a fire, it is often the outer packaging that has taken up a smoky smell. Despite this, the goods contained may be unaffected, having been protected by the outer casing.

To a less scrupulous claimant a fire can be looked on as being an opportunity to get rid of slow-moving and dead stock, turning them into money.

You sometimes find that unaffected goods have been moved into the fire zone to enhance the claim. However, to be successful in this venture it is necessary to understand how a fire works and to consider what happens when a fire occurs in a storage warehouse.

Any fire will draw in a tremendous amount of air,

producing a large upward plume of smoke. When it reaches the roof void it will spread, filling the whole area. When the smoke has nowhere else to go it hits the corners and curls downward towards the floor. Soot on the other hand, being heavier, will fall, rarely drifting far from the fire itself. Hence any goods close to the fire but unaffected by flames or water should be regarded as suspicious.

Old stock has probably been around for some time and is likely to be very dusty. On some occasions it has been possible to take dust samples from such stock and after examination under a microscope, match it with goods from one or more warehouses.

Our comparison tests often proved crucial in our investigations, as in the case of the Kobe cigarettes, described in another chapter, when we were asked to help in a claim for cigarettes stored in a warehouse in Kobe after the 1995 earthquake.

After carrying out a range of tests, comparing with cigarettes on sale in Osaka, there was almost no difference, We were delighted when we heard that the claimant had decided to drop the claim. We had therefore saved the insurer a large amount of money.

Alarming Jeans

We assisted with a claim in the Netherlands about denim jeans in a warehouse next to a building destroyed by fire. Although not directly affected by the fire, the jeans warehouse had been filled with smoke, causing the garments to take up a strong smell of smoke. The claim was for the entire stock on the basis of the goods being unsaleable.

Garments made of denim, having a rough finish and hence a large surface area, are able to pick up smells and taints very quickly. However, by the same token, they can lose these by being aerated. This can be achieved by placing them in fresh air. I was staying in a local hotel and decided to take four pairs of affected jeans to my hotel room to see if they improved overnight.

At about 1.30am the fire alarm in the hotel went off. It eventually stopped, so I opened the door to the corridor to see what was going on, and the fire alarm immediately started again. It was then that I noticed a smoke alarm immediately outside my door. Then the penny dropped: I was the cause. I immediately opened the door to the balcony and placed the four garments in the fresh air, shutting the balcony door. Fortunately it was windy and not raining.

At this point there was a commotion outside. The manager arrived, dressed in his night clothes, apologising to everyone and saying the system had recently been serviced so he could not understand what had happened. To make matters worse, the fire brigade arrived and set up the turntable ladder. Members of crew came to all rooms asking whether occupants were alright. Fortunately, by this time my room was smoke free, so I was in the clear.

On leaving the hotel in the morning with the four pairs of jeans tightly wrapped in newspaper and placed in my luggage, I checked out. The manager offered me a profuse apology for the disturbed night. I thanked him and fled.

18

AEROPLANES

During my travels around Australia, I visited the Croydon Aircraft Company, where they serviced and repaired light aircraft. Many people, particularly farmers in the area, had their own light aeroplanes, some of which were very old. At the time of my visit they were overhauling a de Havilland Dragon, which flew between islands in the 1930s.

There were also a few Tiger Moth biplanes, one of which had lost its entire starboard wing. Its owner had flown into a tree and a new wing was being made for it. I was asked by one chap if I had ever flown in a Tiger Moth. I was able to tell him that I had flown in one many times.

At school we had all been required to join the Combined Cadet Force and for the first three terms we had to be in the Army section. On Field Day each term in the Army section, you had to take part in a mock battle when you would fire blanks. Being the tallest member in our platoon, I was always landed with carrying the Bren gun, whilst others had to carry their 1917 Lee Enfield 303 rifles, which were a lot lighter.

After three months in the Army section, we could transfer to either the Navy or RAF. Having always been interested in boats and ships of all sizes, my first choice might have been the Navy. But school was in landlocked Berkshire and about as far away from the sea as it's possible to be. Rowing a whaler around Frencham Pond did not sound much like fun. So I decided on the RAF.

In this section we would visit a number of RAF stations and on most occasions get a flight. These involved Ansons, Dakotas, Hastings transport planes and Sunderland flying boats.

On one occasion we visited RAF Abingdon where they trained troops of all services to use a parachute. This included jumping from a tower in a parachute harness, and being let down in a controlled way, by a friction roll and learning how to fall on hitting the ground. This experience proved to be good training for my bungee jump in New Zealand decades later.

On one Field Day we visited the Saunders Roe plant in Cowes, Isle of Wight. Their speciality was in building flying boats and they were in the process of building three Princess flying boats. One was complete but without engines.

The Proteus jet-prop engines were not ready at the time of our visit. The design called for 10 prop-jet engines giving a top speed of about 400 mph. These flying boats were huge, with a two-floor configuration, years before the Boeing 747. Only Howard Hughes's Spruce Goose was larger.

Princess flying boats are distinct from seaplanes. The hulls of flying boats sit on the water, whilst seaplanes have two floats that are in contact with the water and attached by legs to the body of the plane. The Princess flying boats could land on lakes, rivers or the sea and the reason for building them was to take passengers to places in the Empire without a suitable airport. They were aimed at the transatlantic market, too, as they could carry 100 passengers in complete luxury. They could also be equipped as troop carriers, carrying as many as three troop ships in a year.

During our visit to Cowes we were given a conducted tour of the aeroplane. It was extremely impressive and provided real luxury, with all passengers having their own cabins. Some time later, the prototype did receive its 10 engines and also its certificate of airworthiness. The plane made a splendid sight flying over Southampton Water.

However, by the time they were ready to fly commercially they had become obsolete. New airports were being opened up around the Empire and new long-haul aircraft were now available. The Princess flying boats never came into service, and were eventually broken up. I thought it was a pity that they were never used on the transatlantic route. They could have had the same effect as Concorde many years later, providing a luxurious way to travel in the early 1950s. I would have liked for one to have been retained as

Princess flying boat

a museum-piece, like Howard Hughes's Spruce Goose in USA. The flying boats had cost £20 million to build in 1950-51 and were sold for scrap a few years later, fetching a mere £18,000.

Taming Tiger Moths

Another good reason for being in the RAF section was that on Saturday afternoons, avoiding games, you could cycle over to RAF Woodley and fly in Tiger Moths or Chipmunks. It was at Woodley airfield in 1931 that RAF flying ace Douglas Bader had the crash that resulted in him having to have one leg removed and the other amputated below the knee. Then, just before the war, Woodley began offering training to young civilians to prepare them for service in the RAF.

Tiger Moth

When we went there in the early 1950s it was an RAFVR (Royal Airforce Volunteer Reserve) station. Many of the pilots were ex-RAF and needed to keep up their hours. Many were rather bored with the whole procedure and welcomed the opportunity to have a new co-pilot. Most of my flights were in Tiger Moths, so I could truthfully tell the man at the Croydon Aircraft Company that I had flown in them many times.

Tiger Moths are bi-planes and originally were used as basic trainers for new recruits in the airforce of many countries. About 9,000 were built for this purpose. The pilot sat in the back seat with the co-pilot or trainee in the front. The seat consisted of a metal scoop and you sat on it with your folded parachute underneath you. Being a bi-plane, it had a tremendous amount of lift. If landing in more than a light headwind, it felt as if it wanted to take off again. You had to be careful with the brakes: if you braked too hard it wanted to tip up. Apart from a joystick, you had foot pedals, a throttle, an altimeter and a compass. The top speed was about 80 mph.

Once airborne, the pilots were usually happy to let the recruit fly the plane. You weren't allowed to take off or land, although I did land on one occasion. It was a still day and he said, "You land it," which I did.

RAF Woodley stopped operating many years ago and is now a housing estate. But I will never forget those Saturday afternoon visits when we were allowed to take to the skies.

No Passport, No Problem

Apart from visiting many parts of Rhodesia during my six years in the country, I was able to visit other countries all over Africa. During my time with the Metal Box Company, representatives from their companies in South Africa, Rhodesia, Kenya and Tanganyika would get together for meetings. In 1965, a representative from the London headquarters joined us in Nairobi, Kenya to visit the respective factories and to discuss common problems or initiatives.

We had one day off, and we all agreed that it be a good idea to charter an aeroplane and fly down to Dar-es-Salaam where none of us had been before. We hired a twin-engined five-seater to carry out the mission. We set off from Wilson airfield in Nairobi and headed south. Fortunately it was a fine day and we had good views of Kilimanjaro and herds of game.

After about one hour the representative from London turned pale and said, "I have forgotten to bring my passport." The Canadian pilot was not at all perturbed and said he could fix it.

Before we reached Dar, he radioed one of his fellow Canadians in the control tower and said, "I have five parcels for you, one is damaged." He was given instructions to taxi into hangar three on landing, then to turn the plane round to face the exit.

"I will arrange for your taxi to meet you in the hanger," said our control-tower contact.

We then had an excellent lunch in Dar-es-Salaam, a city in Africa I had never visited. Afterwards we were given explicit instructions for the return journey.

"The pilot will meet you in hangar three. Please get your taxi to drive into the hangar and then you board the plane as fast as you can."

We roared out of the hangar, took off as fast as possible and all was well. We were airborne before any of the airport's staff realised that anything unusual had taken place. All in all, it was a good day out.

Dar Airport

19

CUBA

I n 2002, my friend Peter and I thought it would be a good idea to spend Christmas in a place new to both of us. We decided on Cuba.

Cuba has had an interesting and varied history. In the 15th century it was colonised by the Spanish, then changed hands a number of times, including three and a half years of American military rule. It gained independence in 1902 and there followed a series of despotic leaders. In 1940 the dictator Batista took control, heading up a corrupt and oppressive regime that lasted until 1959. During his regime, Batista concluded a deal with the USA that Guantanamo Bay could be leased as a base and a prison. The country's main exports were sugar, coffee and tobacco which, along with tourism, made up the majority of its income.

The first leg of our journey was from London to Madrid as there were no direct flights to Havana from Britain at the time. We would then fly with Iberia to Havana, the capital of Cuba. We boarded a Boeing 747, which must have been one

Taxis in Havana

of the originals. It was so old it had the spiral staircase to the top deck that was replaced in later models.

When it was time to take off we taxied out to the runway but did not get very far.

The pilot announced that there was something wrong with the hydraulics and we would have to return to the terminal building. After a two-hour delay we set off again, only to be told that the radio was not working properly and had to be seen to. This was only a short delay of one hour. Then it was the brakes that were not operating properly, resulting in a further two-hour delay. Finally, we were told that all was well, and it was time to take off.

We gathered speed and then, halfway along the runway, there was a loud bang from underneath the plane and we screeched to a halt. One of the cargo doors had blown open. We had to be towed back to the terminal building. It could have been disastrous if this had happened after we had taken off. All things considered, it was a relief to know that we would not, in fact, be travelling on that particular plane. We were told that a relief plane would arrive in the morning and that we would be put up in hotels for the night. All our luggage was taken off the plane and our duty-free items were put in bond.

We were then told that the relief plane would not arrive until the afternoon and then that it wouldn't be arriving at all, as there was no plane available. In the afternoon we returned to the airport and were confronted with the same old banger which they had patched up for our onward journey.

When we eventually – and miraculously – reached Havana, our transport to the hotel in Varadero was not there, presumably it had gone home due to the delay.

There was no sign of our luggage either, as only half of it had been put back on the plane once it had been removed.

We managed to get a lift from another tour operator. At the hotel they said that we did not have a booking and the hotel was full. The first night was spent in a lounge trying to get some sleep. We were eventually given a room in the basement servants' quarters, which were very damp.

There was little good about the hotel. I had heard before we left that you do not expect haute cuisine in Cuba. It was

Our Varadero Hotel swimming pool

true. The food was awful. But the swimming-pool area was alright and drinks were cheap.

I went to look at the beach and was pleased to see that they had windsurfing boards there. When I said I wanted to take one out, I was told that the wind was too strong. This surprised me as the wind could only be described as light. It soon became obvious that the staff simply could not be bothered to rig a board. While the staff were disappointing, the beach itself was excellent, with palm trees and a long sandy shore.

Leaving the hotel on one's own was discouraged, but you could hire a taxi. The taxis were interesting as they were all pre-1959 American limousines because no cars had been imported after the blockade. I was told that they had been given Russian Lada engines.

Our first expedition was a river trip, first in canoes and then on a river boat. We had lunch on board and were entertained by a trio playing local music.

The second was a trip to Havana with a local 'guide'. We had to listen to her telling us what a wonderful man President Fidel Castro was. He had, we were told, seen off the US invasion force at the Bay of Pigs single-handedly in his tank. Said tank is now mounted on a plinth in the city centre. We were also told that 'our leader' had stamped out all forms of prostitution and that anyone involved in it faced a heavy prison sentence.

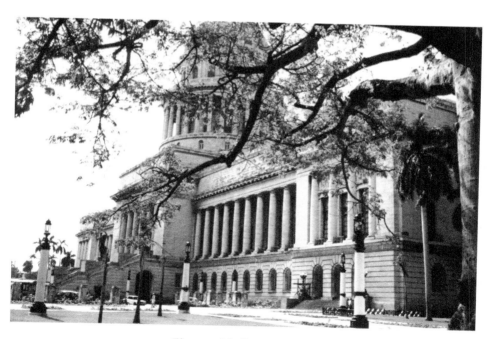

The unused Parliament Building

On the journey into Havana we passed several buildings which were part of the university. We were told that 'our leader' had said that the country could not live on the money from sugar and tourism alone. They had to go high tech. To that end they had started producing proprietary medicines to sell to third-world countries (thereby totally ignoring patent rights).

One of the professors, a 'brilliant' man, had apparently discovered a cure for all cancers. But, when no one would listen to him, he gave himself cancer.

Our 'guide' then said they had another professor who was working on a cure for ageing. I stopped her there and asked about the first professor.

She said that unfortunately he had died, but of influenza, not cancer, you understand. I'm not altogether sure I did.

Our party was given a very good lunch whilst various people told us how good life was in Cuba. Another one gave us a talk on the evils of the USA.

We were then shown round a factory making cigars and another producing rum. We were given a chance to buy some of their products, which turned out to be far more expensive than buying them in local shops.

Although the Cuban hierarchy hated the USA, they certainly capitalised on Ernest Hemingway, the American author and adventurer. We were shown the house where he used to live, his favourite hotel and his favourite bar, where we had to try his favourite cocktail, the mojito. Although the bar was small, there was a trio providing live music.

Everywhere we went there was music. At the supermarket there was a trio at the checkout, on a river cruise there was another. Music could be heard all over the old town. I found it very interesting that the children especially had a natural rhythm about them.

It was dusk when we left Havana in our coach. At traffic lights there were young girls in mini-skirts knocking on car windows and I saw that they were often invited in. I said to our guide, "You said that your leader had stamped out prostitution. That does not seem to be true." She said the girls had been encouraged, after work, to provide a service to help drivers who did not know their way. "I wasn't born yesterday," was my reply.

There were many Canadians staying in our hotel and they were very good company. After the Bay of Pigs fiasco, the US president Kennedy had banned US citizens from visiting or trading with Cuba. He asked Canada to do the same. The Canadian Prime Minister was furious and said that, as a separate country, they would not be told what to do by Kennedy. Cuba, being due south of eastern Canada, had become a very popular place for them to visit. The new terminal building at Havana airport was jointly opened by Canadian Prime Minister Jean Chretian and Fidel Castro in 1998.

During all this time I still had not received my luggage, despite frequent calls to Havana airport. I bought a few basic items of clothing, all of which had been made in the USA. They were imported via the Dominican Republic.

The journey back to Madrid was in a brand new Boeing 747. I came to the conclusion that the old banger we travelled out in had finally expired.

About six months after arriving home, I had a call from Gatwick Airport telling me a suitcase had been found that they thought could be mine. It was.

20

ADVENTURES AFLOAT

The polio I suffered at the age of 12 left me with some difficulties in walking throughout my life. Then, in my seventies, I experienced the condition called post-polio syndrome. I was lucky to have had a mild attack at the time, enabling me subsequently to lead a fairly normal life.

Perhaps because of the limits placed on me by polio, I've always tried to prove that I wasn't a total physical wreck. So as well as doing outlandish things such as bungee jumping in my 60s, I have always tried to stay as active as possible.

Sailing has been a great passion and during my time in Southern Rhodesia I learned to sail a dinghy on the Matopos Dam in Bulawayo. Later on I took up windsurfing, firstly in the Ionian Islands of Greece and then on the Queen Mary Reservoir near Heathrow Airport. The reservoir had the advantage that you could sail all the year round, wearing a wetsuit in summer and a drysuit in winter. During the winter months there were usually fewer people and better winds. At first I found windsurfing impossibly difficult, but with my bullish determination to prove myself, I persevered and I eventually achieved level four.

About 10 years ago I had to give up windsurfing as my balance had completely gone. This was a real blow, but I could, however, continue dinghy sailing.

Most years I went to Salcombe in South Devon to sail dinghies. I found it a good way to get to know friends better. It was impossible to predict in advance how they would behave in a small boat. The winds could be difficult to handle as the hills surrounding the estuary allowed them to come at you at many difficult angles.

I will never forget one long weekend I had there. I took a friend who had been in Rhodesia at the same time as me, although we had never met. I subsequently met her at a London dinner party given by a mutual Rhodesian friend of ours. Her name was Vanessa and we became good friends.

Vanessa was very keen to go sailing on a long weekend in Salcombe. I asked her whether she had done any dinghy sailing before. "Oh yes," she said, "I learnt my sailing in Hermanus in the Cape in South Africa."

I thought that was a good start, so I booked a Wayfarer, a 16ft sailing dinghy, for the weekend. I had also booked into the hotel where I usually stayed.

The following day we went down to start sailing. The wind was about force five, with white tops starting to form on the waves. I asked Vanessa whether she was happy to sail in those conditions. "Oh yes," she said, "I have known far worse in South Africa."

I rowed out to the moored Wayfarer, tied the small rowing boat on to the mooring and started to haul up the sail. I told Vanessa to lean over the bow and be ready to cast off. "As crew you will be manning the jib," I told her.

"What's the jib?" she asked.

I wondered how she could have forgotten that. "What sort of boats have you sailed in South Africa?" I asked.

"Much larger ones than this," she replied, "and with a motor."

It became clear that Vanessa had no experience at all of sailing dinghies. Her sailing experience amounted to her being a passenger in a motor boat with a gin and tonic in one hand.

By this time we were in mid channel with the jib flapping in the wind. "Can we go home now?" said Vanessa. "The wind and rain are ruining my hairdo."

I explained what she should be doing with the jib, but she did not want to know. She just sat in the bottom of the boat and looked miserable.

I had explained to her that if we capsize you must stay with the boat. The lifeboat then passed us on its way out for a practice.

"Who are all those heavenly young men in their mustard suits?" she asked. I explained that she was looking at the lifeboat and its crew.

The wind was picking up and Vanessa asked what I thought the windspeed was now on the Richter Scale. "Those are bloody earthquakes," I snapped, my patience starting to wear thin.

By this time the tide had turned and the main stream was going out fast. I saw we were fast approaching Blackstone Rock at the entrance to the estuary, with the open sea beyond. I managed to bring the boat under the lea of the cliff on which the Marine Hotel is located. We now had some protection from the wind, but we could only make slow progress.

I managed to creep upstream, making a series of small tacks, to our mooring and was passed by the lifeboat returning from its outing. At this point Vanessa suddenly came to life and began waving to its crew. We eventually made it back to the mooring.

I told her I would bring the boat head to wind and drop the main sail. Her job was to lean over the bow, hang on to the mooring and not, on any account, to let go. Vanessa, however, thought it would be easier to lean over the side. We capsized on the mooring, getting the mast stuck in the mud.

I got up onto the dagger board in a vain attempt to right the boat, and shouted at Vanessa to push from her side, but the boat was stuck fast. I called out to her but there was no reply.

For a horrible moment I thought she had been swept out to sea. It was at this point where Rob James, one of Britain's most experienced yachtsmen and well used to ocean sailing, had drowned. Then I saw a bedraggled figure crawling on all fours up the shingle beach. She had abandoned ship.

At that point the lifeboat came to my rescue, pulling me out of the water and putting me in their boat. "If you had stayed in the water much longer you would have got hypothermia," said the captain.

The lifeboat crew then righted the dinghy. Vanessa was not pleased that she had missed out on getting up close with the lifeboat crew. I realised that her idea of a sailing weekend in Salcombe would ideally not involve her leaving the hotel.

On other occasions in Salcombe, when I have taken girls who actually knew how to sail or were keen to learn, I found it to be an enjoyable test of my skills. Having studied the wind speeds and state of the tides, it is a real challenge to sail up the estuary to Kingsbridge and moor up to the Crab Shell Inn. You must then drink at least one pint of beer or scrumpy, (known as the Gurr Tax) and sail back down the estuary before the tide has gone out, leaving you high and dry. This involves making a series of small tacks so that you keep ahead of the ebbing tide.

Cruising

Now that I have had to give up dinghy sailing and windsurfing, I have taken to going on cruises. I have been on small ones with 500 to 700 passengers, to a large one catering for up to 3,500. The contrast between the two sizes is immense.

The bigger cruise ship was very stable in rough weather on account of her size, but involved a lot more walking. Breakfast on the big ship was provided from an all-day buffet where you queue up with a tray. I therefore tended to go to a much smaller restaurant with waiter service.

As is the cruise custom, I had my Christian name pinned to my shirt. I was put at a table with Americans all round me. Filipino crews are usually excellent and this one was no exception. The waiter, seeing I was English and my name being Robin, greeted me as I sat down saying, "Good morning, Sir Robin."

The first American asked me if I was a lord. I said I was not. "But the waiter called you Sir Robin." I explained that the title of Sir would not make me a lord. It would refer to a knight or, less commonly, a baronet. This left them totally confused but still thinking I had a title.

"Would you be an Earl?" asked another.

"No," I said, "I leave those titles to you Americans, such as Duke Ellington, Earl Hynes and Count Basie."

I think he took me literally and said he never knew that.

I was then asked if I had met the Queen of England. "No," I said, "but I have spoken to her on the telephone."

I then had to explain how this had come about. The father of a school friend was the Queen's Press Secretary. It was at the time that Princess Margaret was making up her mind if she could marry Group Captain Townsend. It was not a straightforward question for her because he was divorced. Being in line to the throne and therefore possibly becoming head of the Church of England, marrying a divorcee was out of the question for Margaret. She could have married him, but would have had to renounce her position, her title of Her Royal Highness, her income from the state, plus her Grace and Favour at home.

On that occasion, when I was staying with the Press Secretary and his family, the telephone rang. My friend's father was in the next room pouring drinks and called to me, asking me to answer it for him.

A female voice at the other end of the line said, "Richard?"

"No," I replied and then asked, "Who is that speaking?"

"Get him for me," she said.

I then realised who it was. You do not ask the monarch for his or her name. Once he'd picked up the phone, I overheard my friend's father say, "Good evening, ma'am. Oh, just a young friend of my son's who is staying with us for the weekend."

My second Mediterranean cruise was in a small ship of 500 travellers. The best place to have a drink in the evening was in the Tommy Cooper Bar which had a pianist to entertain us. He told us that previously he had been on the Royal Yacht Britannia. Some of the drinkers said to others that they did not believe him. One of them said, "They would not have had a man like that on the Royal Yacht. He's far too common." Hoping to prove this snob wrong, I said I would find out for them.

During a break in his playing, I bought him a drink and asked him about it. He said he had been a bandsman in the Royal Marines. I asked him whether he had been in the Marine's school of music in Deal, Kent. He said he had, until the IRA had blown it up.

I said I knew someone who had been on the Royal Yacht. He was, in fact, the Surgeon-Admiral and was a near neighbour of mine in London. I asked the pianist if he knew him. He said, "Yes, we all knew David, he was well liked and popular with all on board."

My evidence gathered, I was able to report back that yes, he had indeed been on the Royal Yacht. His critics treated him with more respect after that.

On another occasion I was on one of the smaller ships where frequent travellers got laundry and dry cleaning done, as well as other privileges free of charge.

One woman was furious that, having brought her dining room curtains with her, they had refused to clean them. "After all the money I have spent on this shipping line, they are refusing to dry-clean my curtains," she moaned.

I do not think she realised why we were laughing at her.

Service With a Scowl

Having decided to leave Rhodesia and return to the UK, I thought I would fly to Durban and meet some Voelcker relatives living in Natal whom I had never met. After an enjoyable week's stay I returned to Durban and boarded the SA Vaal, one of the ships that did the mail run to and from Southampton.

The Vaal was previously called the Transvaal Castle and sailed under the Union Castle Line flag. The South African government wanted to own some of the mail boats to sail under their flag. So they asked Union Castle to sell them two of their ships, or they would have to acquire two new ships to operate in competition with them. Union Castle Lines agreed to sell them the Transvaal Castle, now SA Vaal and the Pretoria Castle renamed SA Orangje. They would continue to be operated by Union Castle staff but would now be owned by Safmarine.

We left Durban with the ship only half full. We stopped at Port Elizabeth and East London before arriving in Cape Town. I shall never forget seeing Cape Town and the backdrop of Table Mountain for the first time through a porthole on my cabin. It was a glorious sight. We stayed there for five days and then left for Southampton with the ship completely full.

Apart from passengers, the ship was a bulk wine carrier, and I was told that they made more money out of wine than by carrying passengers. The people onboard consisted of English-speaking South Africans, UK citizens and Afrikaners.

There was quite a bad atmosphere on the ship, but this was not the only problem. At dinner, I was put at a table for eight, who included the First Officer. After one meal he sensibly decided to have all his meals in his cabin.

The waitress gave us all menus, saying she would be back in a moment. When she returned she started to take our orders. Unfortunately, one member of our table, who was in her 80s, was still trying to find her glasses. The waitress did not wait for her to find them, but went off and came back with food for the seven of us. I pointed out that she had not taken the order of the eighth member. "Do you expect me to hang about waiting for her just because she is too slow?" she replied.

I had not met the older lady before, but I knew her daughter and son-in-law in Rhodesia. She was returning to the UK after visiting them. Eventually the waitress returned and was extremely rude to the lady. I told the waitress I would speak to the head waiter if she continued with her rudeness and bad attitude to all of us. It did not get any better.

The head waiter said that there was nothing he could do as she was a member of the Transport and General Workers Union. I pointed out that she was employed by Safmarine/

Union Castle and therefore also had a duty to her employer and to their passengers.

At dinner that evening she asked who had reported her to the head waiter. I said I had, with the agreement of my fellow passengers. She told me to f**k off.

After the meal I went to see the captain. He told me that I was not the only person who had complained about her. He could assure me that she would not be sailing with Union Castle or Safmarine again.

That evening she asked us who had reported her to the captain. I said it was me, explaining that we were fed up with her rudeness and bad service and decided that one of us should complain to the captain. I told her that he had said she would not be sailing again with this ship. Once again she told me to f**k off.

On the final day the waitress was all smiles and I knew why. I said to her, "I am sure you will understand why you are not getting a tip." It was no great surprise to be told once again to 'f**k off'.

Many of the travellers were involved in playing bridge, bingo, Lotto, deck quoits, gambling on the ship's 24-hour mileage and playing with fruit machines. None of these activities appealed to me. I did, however, join a class to improve my dancing. I learned how to do Zorba's dance and a few other useless dances, which I never used again.

I also found some kindred spirits in the Crow's Nest, one of the bars on the top deck that was a sanctuary for UK travellers. I was told by the entertainments manager that I had not signed up for any sporting activities. Under pressure I said I would take part in the table tennis competition. I am glad to say I reached the final and won, beating a rather large and bad-tempered Afrikaner gentleman. That was the limit of my sporting activities on board.

We had two stops on the way, in Gran Canaria and Madeira, reaching Southampton 14 days after leaving Cape Town. I had rather a lot of luggage with me, which had to be weighed before boarding the boat train to Waterloo. To my surprise I was charged £200 for being overweight. It had never occurred to me that there would be a weight limit when travelling on a train. Although the voyage home had not been a great success, I knew that I would return to Africa some time in the future.

21

AT LEISURE

After a busy day it was always nice to go somewhere to unwind with friends. In my early days, from about the age of 18 to 40, I discovered a number of places in London that were quite new to me.

An old school friend took me one evening to the Royal Court Theatre Club. This was situated above the theatre in Sloane Square and was run by writer, chef and raconteur Clement Freud. It was a nightclub that was cheap to enter, as well as serving cheap drinks and food. I could not understand why I had not heard of it before.

I told my friend Anthony that I would love to join the club. At a convenient moment he called Clement over. "My friend Robin would love to join your club," said Anthony.

"Give me one good reason why I should let you in," said Clement.

"Because we both went to the same school," I replied.

"I think that is an excellent reason," said Clement and I was duly admitted.

I realised afterwards that what I had told him was untrue. Clement had been to Saint Paul's School in London, while I had been to Wellington College in Berkshire. However, it was nearly true. Saint Paul's had been evacuated out of London during the war and had been taken in by Wellington.

One of Clement's aims in his club was to give young performers a chance to launch themselves. To start off the evening he told a series of very funny jokes in his deadpan, unsmiling way. This was followed by two or three very nervous young performers who were still polishing their acts.

I will always remember one joke Clement told. It told the story of a woman who went into Fortnum & Mason, the upmarket shop and royal grocer in Piccadilly. She wanted to buy a cauliflower and went to the fruit and vegetable department. She was met by an elegant assistant dressed in a morning tailcoat.

"Can I help you, madam?"

"I wish to buy a cauliflower," replied the woman.

"Certainly, madam, that will be 32 shillings and 10 pence." This translates to roughly £1.70.

"That's outrageous!" exclaimed the customer. "You know what you can do with that."

"I am sorry, madam, I cannot oblige, I am already accommodating a cucumber."

One evening I was contacted by an Irish friend called Maurice. He lived in Dublin, but was in London for a few days and hoped we could meet for dinner. Afterwards he suggested we should go to his club in Soho. It was called the Venus Room and was in Frith Street.

At that time variety theatres were being badly hit by television. Theatres tried to compete by including nudes in their shows. These nudes were not allowed to move. To get round this restriction, strip clubs were opening for members only. As long as it was a members club, show girls could come on and strip off everything.

A new member was supposed to book a week in advance before being allowed to visit. This rule was usually ignored. On my first visit with Maurice I paid the entrance charge, which gave me life membership, and went straight in.

Girls went through their act to an old record player, then left and another girl came on. The girls were shaved, with no body hair. I learned from one of the girls that they were typically earning about £100 per week from performing in the clubs. She said she worked four or five clubs a night. She also told me that her previous job as a typist paid her £4.50 per week. She was planning to make enough money from stripping to be able to afford to buy a flat or house of her own. Then she would give it up.

I returned to the club one evening after attending a wedding. Myself and four other ushers wanted to do something in the evening. I said I was a life member of the Venus Room. So we changed out of our formal clothes and went.

In the club you sat on old tip-up cinema seats, which had seen better days, many having been slashed and with the stuffing hanging out. As one girl was finishing her act, one of our party pulled out some grey stuffing from his chair and went up to the stripper and said, "I think this belongs to you." The whole place dissolved in laughter and the poor, humiliated girl rushed off the stage. The manager appealed for calm and tried to recover the situation. Bouncers then arrived and chucked us out. When we hit the pavement we could hear the other people upstairs still laughing.

I never went back to the Venus Room as a year later Westminster City Council removed their licence for keeping a disorderly house (brothel). I realised that life membership referred to the club's life, not mine, as I had imagined.

At the age of 18 I joined the Berkeley Hotel's young person's scheme. You first had to be vetted by the head waiter, Senor Gabbiati, who decided if you were suitable. The hotel was part of the Savoy Hotel group and was situated on the corner of Berkeley Square and Piccadilly. It should not be confused with the New Berkeley in Knightsbridge. Although it was a popular hotel, particularly with Americans, the dining room was not full during the weekday evenings. They therefore brought in a 'Guinea Pig' scheme whereby young people under the age of 21 could dine and dance as long as they wore a dinner jacket.

The price of a three-course meal was one guinea per head, which included a glass of barely drinkable red wine.

It made an excellent night out and I made good use of it for about five years.

However, at the age of 23, Senor Gabbiati said to me, "Mr Voelcker, you have been 21 for long enough. It is about time you leave the scheme."

Later, I used to frequent the Blue Angel nightclub in Berkeley Square. Leslie Hutchinson (Hutch) played the piano there and sang. I remembered him from my 20s. He was a very good-looking entertainer from Granada who had once been a huge cabaret star and often played at debutante coming-out balls.

When I saw him again at the Blue Angel, he was greatly overweight with white hair and was a heavy drinker. He spent his time being rude to young girls, asking them if they had come in because business was slack on the streets.

I must have been about five times and each time Stirling Moss was there. I never realised how short he was. I suppose this was a good asset if you had to drive a Formula One car.

In the 1970s I went to the Netherlands a number of times with my flatmate Andrew. We stayed with his cousin David who worked for Shell in Den Haag (the Hague). Den Haag is the capital city, although much smaller than the commercial centre, Amsterdam.

There was a magnificent public swimming pool near where David lived and the three of us went there on many of our visits. One day David suggested that, as it was Saturday, we should have an early swim to leave the rest of the day free.

David drove us to the pool but said, at the last minute, he would forego a swim as he was not feeling up to it, but would come back in an hour to pick us up.

Andrew and I entered the pool and went to the changing room. I noticed that the porthole windows of the doors to the pool had been covered over. Being fairly slim in those days I wore a brief pair of Speedos. Andrew, having forgotten to bring his swimming trunks, had borrowed a pair of shorts from his cousin, which extended down to his knees.

We then entered the pool and were confronted by 150 nudists. David had landed us slap bang in the middle of the weekly naturist hour. Everyone in the pool stared at us.

"What do we do now?" asked Andrew. I said, "Either we join them, or we get the hell out of here." I went to have a shower, as required, at the side of the pool, quickly took off my Speedos and jumped in.

Andrew stood there, not sure what to do and then jumped in the pool in his long shorts. People started shouting at him to take them off. I swam up the other end so I was not seen to be associated with him.

The pool attendant called him over and told him to take them off or leave the pool. Suddenly there was a shout from Andrew saying, "They're off!" and he threw his shorts out of the pool. Everyone cheered. The pool was filled with whole families, from children up to their grandparents. Removing my Speedos had produced a great sense of relief. I found that a very odd feeling.

At the far end of the pool area there was a ping pong table where four lads in their late teens were having an unusually enthusiastic game. One of the four seemed to be getting over-excited in full view of everybody, but it did not seem to worry him. Swimmers in the pool gave him a cheer. He turned to face the pool and waved.

When the hour was up we left the pool feeling great. If anyone had asked me if I would like to swim naked I would have refused. Being unknowingly forced to do it, I was very happy to have done so. When David came to pick us up, I accused him of doing it on purpose, but I also thanked him for the experience.

Amsterdam Trip

22

GROUND WORK

Having trained as a soil scientist at Cambridge, I was used on many sites requiring specialist input to assist in rehabilitation or development. One assignment involved the death of some newly planted trees. The site of an old steel works had been acquired by the local authority for transformation into a new forest. About 7,000 young trees were planted. Unfortunately at the end of the season nearly all had died. The local authority tried to sue the landscape architect who had supervised the planting for the loss of the trees.

I visited the site with a tensiometer to determine the moisture content of the soil at various depths below the surface (see photo). It had rained heavily the previous night and hence the ground surface was wet. However, the soil was completely dry beyond the top 2cm. It was easy to determine why the trees had died. A young tree needs watering until it has become established. The site in question clearly had not been watered. Having determined the cause,

Young trees

the question remained as to who was responsible. In the contract for the job it had stipulated that, once the young trees had been planted, the local authority were responsible for the watering. I advised my conclusion to a much-relieved landscape architect.

I was once asked to visit a stately home in South East England known for its magnificent gardens. However, one part of the garden was not performing as well as it should. I visited the site and saw the problem. I subsequently learned that three other consulting firms had looked at the soil problem but could find nothing wrong.

I took soil samples from the surface and at a depth of

New Marina

15cm in the affected areas and also from good growth areas. Analysis showed that the soil texture was suitable and that the major nutrients (nitrogen, phosphorus, potassium, magnesium and calcium) were all present at sufficient levels. Organic matter, pH (acid/alkalinity balance), electrical conductivity (a measure of salinity) and texture were also normal.

To solve the mystery I would have to dig a little deeper. In that part of England, there are many towns and villages with 'hurst' as part of their name, for example Wadhurst, Ticehurst and Hurst Green. I sought to find out why. I found that in such places, the winning of iron had taken place over many centuries. Where you find ironstone you often find manganese associated with it.

Manganese in trace amounts is essential for successful plant growth, but at higher levels it is very toxic. I therefore went back and looked for manganese in the samples I had taken on my visit. Results showed that, in areas where plant growth was normal, manganese levels were satisfactory at pH value of 6.5. However, soil samples from areas showing poor growth had higher levels of manganese. The solution was to raise the pH in the affected soil, which could be achieved by the application of lime to affected areas.

On a different occasion, it was sodium that was causing a problem with the plant life. I was called to a new marina on the south coast. There is always a high demand for marina space and such a development was welcomed in the area.

A bund (embankment) had been constructed from the coast out into the sea using sheet piling (continuous retaining walls). Sea dredging of soil from outside the bund was undertaken to fill it up and the contained water allowed to drain. Once the site had drained sufficiently, work could start in carving out the marina. Planning consent had stipulated that the finished site should contain trees and lawns surrounding houses and other buildings.

The problem was that dredged soil from the seabed contained sufficient salt from the seawater to prevent any plant growth. Apart from preventing plant growth, the sodium in the salt makes the clay very sticky. I lost my boots on many occasions walking round the site.

This problem is also common when farm land becomes flooded with sea water due to exceptionally high tides. The answer is to replace the sodium with calcium, usually in the form of gypsum (calcium sulphate), which is worked into the surface in small applications. If a plentiful supply of fresh water is not available, rain water will remove the sodium, though this takes longer. On a recent visit to the site after about 20 years, I was pleased to see that grass, shrubs and vegetation were well underway.

Sometimes, the solution to non-flourishing plants is very simple, as was the case at the roof garden of The Ismaili Centre in South Kensington. The aim of the building is to be a centre for religious, cultural and social purposes and as a meeting place. It was opened by Mrs Margaret Thatcher

The marina

South Kensington

in April 1985 in the presence of His Highness the Aga Khan, the 49th Imam.

Before the war the site was intended as a home for the Shakespearean Theatre, but after WW2 this project was abandoned when it was realised the site was too small. Now the London headquarters of the Sunni Muslims, it is fairly lavish and has an elaborate roof garden.

We were asked to find the reason why plants on the western side of the building were dying. I looked up the conditions for satisfactory growth of the species involved. My sources of information said that they could not tolerate draughty conditions. The Ismaili Centre is sited on a corner where the Cromwell Road meets Exhibition Road. It turned out to be one of the most draughty places in the area. My advice was to replace them with a draught-tolerant species.

Molotov Cocktails

Occasionally, my experiences of living through the war were of great help in my work. Following our defeat at Dunkirk, although about 333,000 troops were rescued, we had to leave behind all our fuel and weapons. This left existing troops in the UK with very few weapons. A call went out to anybody who had rifles or sporting guns to hand them in to the police for the duration of the war. My own father handed in his sporting gun and was given a receipt to be redeemed after the war.

Dad's Army-style volunteers had to come up with methods of fighting if the Germans had invaded. There were many ways invented to produce Molotov Cocktails, involving a range of chemicals. The one I remember best consisted of a beer or milk bottles, filled with benzene and white phosphorus, sometimes containing some rubber to make it sticky. When the phosphorus was exposed to the air as the bottle was thrown and broken, it burst into flames and dense white smoke of phosphorus pentoxide (P_2O_5) was emitted.

On three occasions I was asked by clients to inspect sites required for development. They had started site surveys using a JCB digger but the dug holes had burst into flames and white smoke had been emitted. Being old enough to remember WW2, I knew exactly what the problem was.

Developers of all three sites were keen to start work without delay. I knew that, if Health and Safely were called in, it would have taken a long time to get the go-ahead. Having trained as a soil scientist I knew that P_2O_5 was not only inert, but it was also phosphorus, a plant nutrient. The way to deal with the problem was simply to reassure the neighbours that the rather alarming white cloud coming towards their washing was not actually dangerous or harmful to health. I had three very relieved clients.

Ducks Stop Play

John Paul Getty Jr was immensely rich, like his better-known father. He bought a rundown stately home in Buckinghamshire as his base when in the UK. In later life he became fascinated with the game of cricket, having been introduced to the game by Mick Jagger. He was keen to become a member of the Marylebone Cricket Club (MCC), the most prodigious cricket club in England. At the time the MCC were raising money to rebuild the Mound stand at Lords. Getty provided a large sum of money towards its cost and was immediately made a member of the club.

The cricket pitch

JP Getty Cricket Pitch

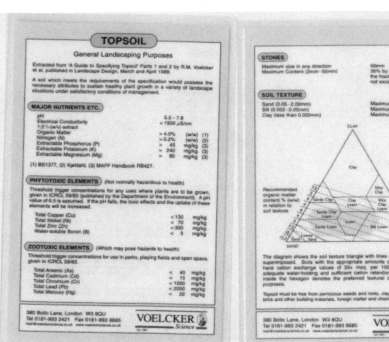

Cricket

Getty's interest in cricket went even further. He wanted a full-sized cricket field constructed at his Buckinghamshire home. The ideal spot was located and a contractor employed for its construction.

The site consisted of compacted chalk over a covering of top soil. Chalk is usually free draining, but the degree of compaction was so severe that it was almost impermeable and very slow to drain. We were contacted by the site manager, who said there were ducks swimming over the playing surface. He was seeking our help to find a rapid solution to fix the problem, preferably before the inaugural match in about four weeks' time. Former PM John Major had accepted an invitation to attend.

We used a technique called sand slitting, whereby a series of slits are made in the ground down to less compacted soil. These slits are then filled with sand, providing an exit route for surface water. This provided a temporary solution to the problem and the match went ahead as planned. However, a really more sophisticated form of drainage was required as a permanent solution. Mole draining was recommended. This method is suitable for clay soil and heavily compacted soils, requiring a machine for drilling holes through the chalk (see picture).

Mole draining

The Royal Agricultural Society

Starting with my great grandfather, Dr Augustus Voelcker, male members of my family have been associated with the Royal Agricultural Society (RASE) since its inception. Dr Voelcker was appointed to be their Agricultural Chemist, and also to set up and run their laboratory in London.

He also set up the original work at Rothamsted Agricultural Research Station. He was convinced that potassium was a major essential plant nutrient, along with nitrogen and phosphorus and set out to prove it. He not only proved it, but at the same time discovered cation-exchange capacity (CEC). This is the ability of plants to retain nutrients so they are not washed out of the soil when it rains.

He added successive amounts of potassium fertiliser to the soil and sampled drainage water to see how much was being washed out. To his amazement none came out. Back in the laboratory he replicated the experiment and found there was something else instead in the water. It was the ammonium ion. Clearly the potassium ion had knocked some of the ammonium ions from the soil lattice.

Clay has a high CEC, silt has less and sand almost none. Organic matter also has a high CEC. This is shown on the diagram of a laminated card we used to give to clients. The triangular soil texture diagram is the one used by the United States Department of Agriculture and widely adopted.

In 1863 Dr Voelcker set up the consultancy that bears his name. After his death, he was succeeded by one of his sons, Dr John Augustus Voelcker, who carried on his father's work at the consultancy. My father, Eric, his nephew, worked with his uncle, taking over full control of the practice following his uncle's death in 1937.

All of the above relatives were appointed agricultural consultants to the RASE. However, times were changing, RASE members were less likely to be required or paid for their services, which were being provided free by the National Agricultural Advisory Service (NAAS) and its successor the Agricultural Development Advisory Service (ADAS).

In 1989 the RASE was celebrating its 150th anniversary. Our consulting practice, the name now shortened to Voelcker Science, was invited to have a stand in the Hall of Science into Practice, free of charge, in recognition of our 130 years association with the RASE.

I was told that the Duke of Edinburgh would be visiting all the stands in the Hall. Before his arrival, I was asked by some committee members if I knew how to address royalty, which I did. When His Royal Highness arrived I was amazed that he had done his homework and knew all about us. He first appeared to be rather brusque but very much to the point.

His first question to me was, "Why did they sack you?" I explained that times had changed and we now did a lot

more than just agricultural science. We were very much
involved with the environment and food safety. The Duke
then pointed to a picture of a girl, one of our microbiologists,
who was examining a ready meal.   "What's she doing?"
he asked, looking mystified.

"Well, sir, she is examining a ready meal, the sort of food
you or I would buy in Tesco's and put in the microwave." He
still looked blank and then laughed. I thought, What am I
saying? He probably has no experience whatsoever of either
Tesco's or a ready meal.

In all we had about five minutes together. Next to our
stand there was an enclosure containing llamas, which
were being shown as an alternative to the more common
indigenous ones. They are an excellent source of protein
and also some valuable wool. Unfortunately, the llamas were
continually breaking wind.

"Was that you?" asked the Duke.

"No sir," I replied and we both laughed.

Prince Philip, Duke of Edinburgh

The Bath and West of England Society

As well as working for the RASE, my family predecessors had also been consultants to the Royal Bath and West of England Society. This society pre-dates the RASE and survives successfully to the present day by being a society for not only farming but also manufacturers.

I arranged to meet the secretary, a very pleasant ex-Army man, to tell him about the family's connections with the society. He told me that, only recently, the committee had discussed the idea of appointing someone since the post had been vacant for some time. It had decided to offer me the post of Honorary Consulting Chemist, which I readily accepted.

In 1854 the Society had appointed my great-grandfather, Augustus Voelcker, to be its Consulting Chemist. It was gratifying to be following in the steps of my great-grandfather. The position was unpaid but was extremely valuable in contacting prospective clients and seeing existing ones. It was also very quotable when tendering for projects in any fields we undertook.

At that time our work was largely based on services to the agricultural industry. Today the present owners of the practice provide a wider range of services, helping clients in the food industry at the pre-production stage (labelling and legislation), during production (quality control) and post-production (shelf-life studies).

We took a stand at the annual Bath and West of England Show for a number of years. We also sponsored the English wine, Pavilion. In those days the duty on English wines was far above that of continental wines and its quality was very variable. Today English wines have come a long way, particularly with white and sparkling wines. I suggested to one cider maker that he should consider producing English Calvados, i.e. Apple Brandy. In the past it had been made in the UK under the name of Apple Jack. In England we only make one spirit, gin, and I thought it would be nice to have another one.

In 1999 we sold the consultancy practice to one of the privatised water companies and they decided to cut our links with the Royal Bath and West of England Society.

Dr. Voelcker

THE ROYAL BATH AND WEST OF ENGLAND SOCIETY

EDMUND RACK · FOUNDER

1777

Royal Bath Logo

23

THE PACIFIC ISLANDS

I was a consultant to an international firm of loss adjusters who wanted a scientific brain to assist them in judging the validity of certain claims. I received an urgent message saying could I go to Bangkok as soon as possible to assist with a claim from an international firm making detergents, shampoos and cosmetics. I booked the first flight I could.

Bangkok is the capital city of Thailand with a population of over 11 million people. This was my first visit. On visiting places for the first time I always like to learn about their history. I discovered that the country was formerly known as Siam. It is bounded by Myanmar (formerly Burma), Laos, Cambodia and Malaysia. It is a constitutional monarchy with parliamentary democracy, although it has been subjected to military-led coups recently.

The country has never been colonised directly, apart from a takeover by the Japanese during World War Two. In the last century, the country was under pressure from both

Britain and France and conceded territory to both. France obtained territories in French Indo-China, increasing the sizes of Vietnam, Cambodia and Laos considerably. Britain gained territory in the north to Burma and to Malaya in the South.

The factory I had to visit was about 30 miles east of the city. An early start was necessary to miss the worst of the traffic. Even so, it still took about three hours each way to cover the 30 miles. A warehouse where raw materials were stored had been damaged by fire. They wanted to find out how much of the stored materials had been damaged and if any could be used.

I first saw the main factory where various items were produced. They were particularly worried about a machine that packed hair shampoo into plastic sachets. Each roll of plastic made eight sachets. The ends of the roll, sachets one and eight, had suffered smoke damage in the fire, while the others appeared to be unaffected.

I took samples of both the end and middle sachets and submitted them to a microbiological examination. Fortunately they had an in-house laboratory for this purpose. The results showed that sachets from two to seven were usable whereas the outside sachets, one and eight, were unusable. It was a simple matter to cut off the end rows, saving 75 per cent as usable. There were many other materials to go through. Fortunately much of it could be used.

This particular claim was sufficiently large for the area manager of the loss adjusters, who covered much of the Pacific, to fly up to Bangkok from his base in Melbourne, Australia. He said he would normally visit Bangkok routinely about twice per year, but a claim like this was big enough for a special visit. I liked Patrick a lot and he seemed very competent in this job.

The manager of the insured took us out to dinner. Afterwards he asked if anyone would like to visit Patpong. I did not know what he meant. He explained that it was the Red Light area. Apart from being intrigued, I thought it would be rude to say no.

We started off in Patpong One, this was the straight one. There was a raised dais in the middle of the area on which paraded a slow-moving number of girls wearing not more than a g-string, a number and a few sequins.

I asked Patrick if he frequented these places on his visits. "No, in my younger days, before I was married, I did. But I am now happily married with two teenaged boys."

We watched as girls paraded slowly in front of us, each one trying to catch our eye. One of the girls saw the Aussie and clearly recognised him. She jumped down and said to him, "Patrick you did not tell me you were coming back this week."

I looked at him and he said, "Well, perhaps once or twice, mate." He was totally unfazed at being caught out.

I had a chance to talk to the girl. She was obviously

A GOOD LIFE

intelligent and spoke good English. She was from the north of the country which is a very poor, agricultural area. She said she was only doing this to make enough money to go to university. Her parents could not afford to do this. I wished her luck.

We were then taken to Patpong Two where a similar performance was taking place. Our host asked what I thought. Apart from saying very nice, I commented that they were taller than the first lot, but I knew they weren't lady boys, who tend to be much shorter. "You are right, look at their Adam's apple and bums," he said. I then saw what he meant. They were all transvestites.

"Anyone want to see Patpong Three?" said our host. I asked what happened there. "It's the gay one." We decided to give it a miss.

The surrounding country around Bangkok is also worth a visit. A trip up the river in a long boat is an experience not to be missed. The boats are powered by old lorry diesel engines from which the gear boxes and exhaust systems have been removed. In their place, a long drive with a propeller have been fitted over the back of the boat. The engine is fitted so that the propeller and shaft can be raised or lowered into the river. When it is lowered the boat takes off fast and is extremely noisy. To slow down or stop, the engine is lowered so that the propeller is out of the water.

Some of the canals off the main river have floating markets. Goods are sold from boats on which whole families live and most are very colourful. For travelling round the city, a ride in a tuktuk is an interesting experience that tests one's nerves. Drivers seem to be able to get through jams much quicker than a real taxi. Some of the more expensive hotels do not like tuktuks arriving at their main entrances, so the driver leaves you to get out in the road and walk the last bit of the journey.

The city's road system has been gridlocked with appalling traffic jams as long as I can remember. As a pedestrian, I had great trouble negotiating the traffic. Thankfully, my new Aussie friend Patrick taught me was how to cross a busy Bangkok street with moving traffic in both directions. You look determined, put your hand up and walk. Somehow the traffic is able to miss you. Before that, I had stood on the pavement waiting for a gap in the traffic that never came and eventually gave up.

The railway system is not good but is being upgraded. At present, the way south only goes as far as Wua Hin, about one third of the way to Singapore. The existing system is very slow with frequent stops. An up-to date local and long distance railway system will be welcomed. New lines are being constructed and a new multi-storey central station is being built in Bangkok.

In the early part of the 20th century, a British engineer persuaded the King to allow the train line to be established further south through the Malay Peninsula to Kuala Lumpur and on to Singapore. However the King insisted that a special station be constructed at Hua Hin for himself and his family so that they would not have to mix with the common people. Travelling first class in the Eastern and Oriental train from Bangkok to Singapore is one of the great train journeys of the world.

During the six years I lived in Brisbane I took advantage of its position on Australia's east coast. It was an ideal starting point to visit some of the islands in the South Pacific. Fiji was one of the countries I was keen to visit and I went there many times.

Fiji consists of about 300 islands and is part of Melanesia, which also includes Vanuatu, Papua New Guinea and

Me at the Royal Palace Bangkok

the Solomon Islands. Fiji's principal island is Viti Levu, where 75 per cent of the people live, mostly in coastal areas. Its capital is Suva. The second-largest place is Nadi (pronounced Nandi).

Fiji has had a difficult time over the years due to tribal warfare. In 1865 the warring factions agreed on a truce but this was short-lived. In 1874, a meeting of chiefs thought the best way out of their problems was to approach the United Kingdom and, as a result, it became a British colony.

Sir Arthur Gordon, the first British governor, was keen to develop the country's economy and started by inviting an Australian sugar producer for help in setting up sugar plantations. The first one opened in 1882 and by 1889 there was a need to bring in outsiders to work in the sugar plantations. Over 60,000 Indians were brought in and currently their descendants make up about 45 per cent of the Fiji population.

At one stage in recent years, Asians outnumbered the indigenous people, which was one of the reasons for coups taking place. Some of the Indians felt it was not safe to remain and relocated to India. This move allowed the indigenous population to regain the majority, having exceeded 51 per cent. Today, the Indians run most of the industry and commerce.

By the 1960s people started asking for independence from Britain and in 1974 Fiji became an independent republic. However, the country was not free from feuding between the various racial and political factions. There followed a number of coups and counter coups.

I looked up on the UK Foreign Office website to see if it was safe to visit. It said it was risky and better to go somewhere else. I repeated the exercise on the Australian website. It said, 'No worries mate. Go there and have a good time.'

My first visit to Fiji was just after a coup. At the time, the president (indigenous) controlled the army whilst the police came under the control of the prime minister (Indian). The president sent the army to every police station and removed their weapons, effectively winning the battle.

On my visits to Fiji I stayed at the Warwick Hotel on the Coral Coast. It was an excellent hotel with a large range of activities and facilities. I had my last windsurfing holiday there, keeping inside the coral reef.

I decided to see more of the island so I took a trip eastward to a river that led to an internal part of the island. There were about 30 of us on the trip. We transferred from our bus to the two long boats that would take us on a trip upstream to a village. The boat trip itself was interesting as we passed through heavily wooded land on both banks consisting mainly of huge bamboo trees.

After an hour and a half we arrived at the village but were not allowed off the boats until we had elected one of our number to be the visiting chief. In the end I was appointed to lead our team.

The visit started with us being shown around the village, which was very impressive. They were totally independent of the outside world, producing all their own food. In the school house the children were well behaved and learning to use computers. Electric power was provided by a wind generator.

After our visit we entered the marae (a meeting house) to meet the chief and elders. They were dressed in white grass skirts. The men in our party were told to sit on chairs. I, being our chief, had to sit out in front facing their chief. Our women had to stand at the back.

We started by drinking Kava. This drink was prepared by various herbs and roots being covered with water in a wooden bowl. The contents were kneaded by each of the elders, and then the chief was asked to taste it. The resulting product consisted of a rather unpleasant brown liquid.

The chief tasted the Kava for his approval followed by all the elders. The bowl was then passed to me to taste. It did not taste too bad, but a short while later my tongue went numb. The bowl was then passed to the men in our party, but the women weren't allowed to taste it. The bowl came back to me, and I had to finish the dregs.

We then had a speech of welcome from their chief and they all looked at me to say a few words. I said how pleased I was to have this opportunity to visit a part of Fiji I had not

The Author in Fiji

been to before. I thanked them for all for their hospitality.

I then remembered that Fiji had recently won the Hong Kong Sevens (seven-a-side rugby) and congratulated them for it. One of the Aussies called out to me, "You got that one right, mate, for once."

We then had a magnificent feast where we all had to sit cross-legged on the floor. After an excellent visit we all proceeded back to our boats and headed back to the real world.

Back in the hotel each evening there was an organised activity on which you could bet. The first evening it was frog racing. They were, in fact, cane toads with numbers painted on their backs. The next night they had the hairy chest competition (men only). It turned out to be an excellent trip and a worthwhile visit to a fascinating country.

Western Samoa

I had always wanted to go to Samoa having heard much about it from my father. His brother, my Uncle Frank, had helped to steer the country to independence from Britain. Frank had fought in the Great War and eventually transferred from the British to the New Zealand Army after meeting and marring a Kiwi girl. He became a well-known figure in New Zealand and was eventually made Administrator of Western Samoa.

The country had been a German colony up to 1914,

leaving behind a brutal reputation. In 1914 at the start of the Great War, the British Government asked New Zealand to kick the Germans out of the country. They did not want it being used as a base to sink British shipping in the South Pacific. The Kiwis did an excellent job, removing the Germans without a shot being fired. It then became a British colony, administered by New Zealand.

Demands for independence began in the 1920s and 1930s but discussions were put on hold due to the war. After the war, demands for independence started again, with politicians referring to Tonga, which had just been granted independence.

My uncle was asked by the New Zealand Government to become the administrator and investigate these demands. If they were genuine, he was asked to come up with a workable plan to satisfy both the Chiefs, who had the power, and the people, who wanted the vote. The plan he introduced was accepted and allowed everyone to have the vote, but only chiefs could stand for parliament.

Samoa had two notable residents, author Robert Louis Stevenson and hotelier Aggie Grey. Aggie Grey's father was English and her mother was Samoan. Her mother died early and she was brought up by her father and stepmother. Aggie decided to set up a hotel and give it her name. Aggie Grey's hotel became world famous and many notable people stayed there, including Robert Morley, Gary Cooper, Noel Coward, William Holden and Marlon Brando. Rumour had

Valima House

it that the hotel also became famous among sailors, many of whom made a detour there to enjoy the female company it provided.

Aggie was very friendly with James A Mitchener who wrote the book Tales of the South Pacific on which the stage play and musical South Pacific were based. It was said that the role of Bloody Mary in the musical was based on Aggie Grey. She died in 1988. When I stayed in the hotel it was very run down but steeped in history. It is now part of the Sheraton chain.

Whilst I was there I saw some Samoan cricket. It was quite unlike any cricket I have watched or played. The playing surface is 22 yards of concrete, the wickets are much taller than ours but with no bales and the bats are more like baseball bats. The number of players is variable as long as each side has the same number.

One of the most popular tourist attractions on Samoa is the Robert Louis Stevenson Museum. This was the Scottish-born author's home for four years and it is where he died at the age of 44. He suffered from ill health all his life, in those days it was known as consumption. He tried living in a number of locations that would be beneficial to his health and finally settled on Samoa. He built a large house there, called Vailima, which looked as if it would be more at home in London's home counties. Stevenson had become rich and famous through writing books such as Treasure Island, Kidnapped and Jeckyll and Hyde. He was well loved by the Samoans and both he and Aggie Grey have featured on Samoan stamps.

More recently, Western Samoa has decided to drive on the left to be in keeping with Australia and New Zealand. It has also moved the International Date Line to the west of the country from the east. It is now the first country in the world to start the New Year.

Aggie Grey's Hotel

Dining Room

Vanuatu

Vanuatu is a group of islands in the South Pacific Ocean, inhabited by the indigenous Melanese people. It was formerly called New Hebrides, thanks to Captain Cook who came up with the name when he landed on one of the islands in 1774.

In the early seventeenth century, Spanish adventurers occupied much of Vanuatu. Then, in the nineteenth century France and Britain claimed parts of the country, eventually setting up a joint government which they called a Condominium. It was not a great success. The Condominium (which came to be known as the Pandemonium) had immense problems. It proved difficult for the two countries to agree on anything, including which side of the road cars should drive on, which legal system should be used, which country should provide the judges, the jail staff. In the end two jails were built and there were two sets of police.

In the early 1970s an independence movement was formed which resulted in the country gaining independence in 1980. The country became the Republic of Vanuatu, much to the relief of everybody.

During World War Two the Americans built an airfield on Espiritu Santo Island as part of the fight against the Japanese. The Americans brought their money, which acted like a shot in the arm to the local economy. It also brought resentment to the local population who were desperately poor and wanted to live like the Americans. When you visit the site of the airfield there are people selling souvenirs, such as 50-year-old Coca Cola bottles and parts of old aeroplanes. The main income to the country is from the tourist trade. Apart from that, the country is dependent on grants from UK, France, the UN and others.

Pentecost Island is well known for the local bungee jump. In fact, this is where the idea for the modern bungee jump in New Zealand originated. After puberty, lads do the jump to prove their manly qualities. First a wooden tower is built to jump off and each lad has to cut a vine that will support his weight and is the right length to stop him

Vanuatu

hitting the ground. The jump is done almost naked.

In modern bungee jumping the rubber rope is flexible, allowing the jumper to bounce a number of times. On Pentecost Island, however, the vine does not give, so the jumpers are pulled up short. If the vine is too long, it usually results in death when the jumper hits the ground. A number of young girls watch from the ground looking up in admiration at these brave lads.

When I was in Vanuatu, a successful jump had to be made before a jumper could join a tribe, or get married. The tribe that takes them will accept them based on the size of their genitals. Those who are not well endowed often cut and shape a piece of bamboo which, when worn, makes them look much bigger than they really are. Although I did a bungee jump in New Zealand, it is difficult to imagine what these lads go through mentally and physically before and during this death-defying activity.

Although a very poor and underdeveloped country, Vanuatu is well worth a visit.

Bungee jumping on Pentecost Island

Bungee jumping on Pentecost Island

LAST WORD

All in all I have had a good life and have done much and achieved many things. I have always been keen on travelling and have visited over 60 countries, working in many of them. I always found it interesting to see different customs and traditions.

Whilst I initially made a good recovery from poliomyelitis contracted at the age of 12, I have been left in later life with difficulty in walking. However, I keep the upper body strong through exercise. One never knows what is around the corner health wise, but I will be satisfied if the old brain keeps working.

One of the main problems as you get older is loneliness as you lose old friends and find it difficult to replace them.

I have been asked how I view the future. Being in my 86th year, I do not think it is possible to anticipate the future. For the time being I am keeping myself busy writing a second book, which will complement this one.

Thank you for reading my book.
Robin Voelcker

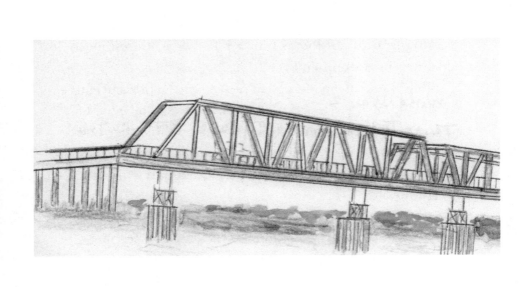

ACKNOWLEDGEMENTS

I would like to thank a number of people who have provided help and encouragement to me in writing this book. These include Ceri MacKellar, a fellow author in South Africa and Liz Billingham, a former director of one of the large publishing house's subsidiaries.

There are others who have experienced some of the tales with me around the world, and others who have read relevant chapters and given me advice and suggestions. These include Nick Billingham, Colin Bungay, Fiona Towse, Eilean Gilmour, Jacek Chudy, Christie Griffiths and Debbie Emerson.

I would also like to thank my computer experts, Francesco Braun, Neil Mason, Christie Griffiths and Bob Gould. They completed this work rapidly and accurately, with a skill far beyond anything I could have done.

Finally, I would like to thank Aileen O'Brien and Beth Williams of StoryTerrace for help and guidance in making this book happen.

StoryTerrace

Printed in Great Britain
by Amazon

66148808R00169